ANOTHER WAY

BUILDING
COMPANIES
THAT LAST . . .
AND LAST . . .
AND LAST

ANOTHER WAY

DAVE WHORTON
WITH **BO BURLINGHAM**

HARVARD BUSINESS REVIEW PRESS • BOSTON, MASSACHUSETTS

This work depicts actual events in the life of the author as truthfully as recollection permits and/or can be verified by research. Occasionally, dialogue consistent with the character or nature of the person speaking has been recreated to the best of the author's ability. All persons within are actual individuals; there are no composite characters.

The web addresses referenced in this book were live and correct at the time of the book's publication but may be subject to change.

Cataloging-in-Publication data is forthcoming.

ISBN: 979-8-89279-113-7
eISBN: 979-8-89279-114-4

The paper used in this publication meets the requirements of the American National Standard for Permanence of Paper for Publications and Documents in Libraries and Archives Z39.48-1992.

Dave Whorton

*To Burt McMurtry, my wise mentor and friend,
who passed in 2018*

*To Lisa, my wife, for her courage to do it differently
and reject status games*

*To Briggs and Rylee, my kids—and to the generations
ahead who will own Evergreen companies—may you enjoy
the shade of the trees we plant today, steward them well,
and plant many more*

Bo Burlingham

*To my wife, Lisa, the love of my life, who has kept me going
for more than fifty years, and to Jake and Maria,
Kate and Matt, Owen, Kiki, Fiona, and Jack, because they
make it all worthwhile*

CONTENTS

PART THREE

THE EVERGREEN ADVANTAGE

PREFACE

I first heard about Dave Whorton from his erstwhile partner Chris Alden, who was working with him to set up Tugboat Institute, a membership organization for the leaders of companies that Dave had named "Evergreen" companies.

I was editor-at-large of *Inc.* magazine at the time, as well as cofounder of the Small Giants Community, based on a book I had written titled *Small Giants: Companies That Choose to Be Great Instead of Big.* There was some obvious crossover in our thinking, I would learn, as Evergreen companies practice Paced Growth as one of their seven core principles. Alden thought some members of my Small Giants Community might be interested in attending their upcoming conference in Carmel-by-Sea, California.

I couldn't attend the conference, but I was fascinated by the concept, especially given its unlikely origin in Silicon Valley, the last place you'd expect to find any interest in private companies that eschewed venture capital and never intended to be sold or taken public. I resolved to find out more with the intention of possibly writing an article on the phenomenon.

Toward that end, I introduced myself to Dave on his turf in Palo Alto, in mid-December 2014. We chatted about the Evergreen companies that attended his first two gatherings, and they sounded a lot like some of the companies I had met through *Inc.* and my research on *Small Giants*, including one that I knew particularly well, namely SRC Holdings—formerly Springfield

Remanufacturing Corp.—of Springfield, Missouri, with whose cofounder and CEO, Jack Stack, I had written two books. I suggested that Dave read the first of those books, *The Great Game of Business*. A couple of weeks later I was surprised to learn that, after my interview, not only had he read the book, but he'd arranged to visit Stack in Springfield.

I continued to do research for an article on Evergreen companies and Tugboat. Among other things, I attended the next Tugboat Institute Summit in Sun Valley, Idaho, where—at Whorton's invitation—I had agreed to give a brief talk about my latest book, *Finish Big: How Great Entrepreneurs Exit Their Companies on Top*. That experience gave me a better sense of the organization he was building and the founders and business leaders he was attracting. I was most struck by their determination to build companies that would last much longer than they themselves would be around to participate in. I decided to make that the focus of my article for *Inc*. My editors loved the idea, and I thought they would make it the cover story.

But as the publication date approached, I was told that the magazine had a "scoop" that it would have to give priority on the cover instead. The scoop turned out to be what my editor said was an "exclusive" interview with Elizabeth Holmes, the founder and CEO of Theranos, manufacturer of a supposedly revolutionary new blood testing system. Sure enough, the October 2015 issue appeared with Elizabeth Holmes on the cover portrayed as "The Next Steve Jobs." Also mentioned on the top right of the cover was my story about building companies that would last a hundred years.

Two weeks later, the *Wall Street Journal* published the first of John Carreyrou's exposés about Elizabeth Holmes and the Theranos fraud, for which she was ultimately convicted and sent to prison. My article about Tugboat Institute held up considerably better.

Thereafter I continued to follow Dave Whorton and Tugboat Institute's growing membership and attended most of his gatherings every year. I continued to be very impressed by the company leaders whom I met there—their humility, the lengths to which they went to support their people, the role that they played in their communities, their attention to the quality of the products and services they offered their customers. I included several of their companies in the monthly column I was then writing for *Forbes*.

It occurred to me that a much wider audience would like to hear the story of Tugboat Institute and how a venture capitalist like Whorton wound up starting it. These Evergreen companies constituted, after all, an important part of the American economy that had heretofore completely escaped the notice of the wider business community. When Dave happened to mention that people had suggested he write about the subject, I jumped at the chance to volunteer my services. And that's how this book came to be written.

What interested me most in working on the book was the opportunity it involved to examine two totally different concepts of business—or actually three, if you consider that Kleiner Perkins exposed him to two ways of building companies with venture capital. All three ways can produce significant companies. The path founders choose depends in large part on their purpose, values, ego needs (including validation), and goals. Dave Whorton believes that the best businesses will do what Bill Hewlett and David Packard had done with their company in its first three decades under their leadership—that is, build a company without outside funding that not only makes great products for customers and contributes to some greater good, but fosters better lives for the people who do the work required (thereby also contributing to that greater good). Dave's experience and the open access to his community of Evergreen companies gave me new insights into how that is done and specifically how they go about it.

My hope is that readers will appreciate the role of those companies not only in shaping our economy but in enriching our world. I also hope that readers who have their own businesses or are contemplating starting a new business will see the Evergreen company model as one worth pursuing themselves.

—Bo Burlingham
September 2024

Introduction

Today, I find many people discouraged, if not angry, about capitalism, our government institutions, and our future. This book is meant to be a salve of sorts, a vehicle to tell you about good things happening out there. *Another Way* is my attempt to build awareness and celebrate an underappreciated and undersupported category of values-driven companies that are humbly and steadfastly making significant contributions in our communities, and plan to do so for decades, sometimes centuries, going forward. These companies, and there are many of them, represent capitalism at its best.

I was first exposed to this kind of company through my first real job at Hewlett-Packard when I was sixteen. (Prior to that job, my enterprises consisted of two newspaper routes, mowing lawns, trading Atari 2600 cassettes, and even a stint in commodities as I traded silver coins and bars; I enjoyed making money and the freedom it offered me.)

Over four summers working at three different HP factories in Sonoma County, California, I earned the money that helped pay my way through the University of California, Berkeley, where

I studied mechanical engineering. Crucially, my time in these factories taught me about the "HP Way," specifically, Bill Hewlett and Dave Packard's belief that if you take care of your people, they will take care of everything else. These two founders made an indelible mark on me.

My career took me eventually to the heart of Silicon Valley—working alongside the most influential power brokers at the most influential venture capital firm, at the height of the Valley's emergence as the epicenter of tech innovation. Later, I'd work at a top-five private equity firm. Along the way, I'd found two high-profile VC-backed companies. One went public and one was sold for a half-billion dollars. It was a heady time.

I'm burnishing my résumé quickly here not out of vanity but because I've come to realize that my experiences have given me a unique perspective on this engine that has driven business and innovation for more than a quarter-century now. I was there at the start of a tectonic shift in how we think about the value and purpose of a business. I saw what it became, and how it evolved into something far different and far less appealing than what it was when I started. I felt the same things you do, the discouragement, the exasperation (and for many, the anger), the sense that capitalism has run amok.

What's been celebrated and amplified in that time is the de facto get-big-fast model that evolved into a growth-at-all-costs model adopted by angels and venture capitalists since Netscape's blockbuster IPO; the downsizing of workforces by private equity firms gobbling up companies fueled by trillions in debt and equity (mostly from pension funds, ironically); a celebrity culture of outsized personalities admired for, as much as anything, garnering conspicuous personal wealth using this system.

Silicon Valley has, over that time, lost its soul. But I never completely forgot the HP Way even if it's a relic of an earlier Valley with a different purpose. I knew, even as I worked in the VC and startup machine, that we had lost something important about the role of values-driven, enduring-growth companies in our society.

So, I went looking for some. What I slowly uncovered would astonish me. It would dismantle my worldview, built up over more than two decades in the Valley, and replace it with something so alien to anyone entrenched on Sand Hill Road that at times it seemed impossible to believe. Not only were there companies out there like Hewlett-Packard in its heyday, or even more impressive, but they could be found in almost every industry, at almost every size, under multiple ownership types, and across many generations. One of those firms is almost three hundred years old. They all perform extremely well; they weather hard times better; they build deeply happy and loyal workforces; they are quiet pillars of their communities; they make good money. Few people in esteemed business circles seemed to know about them, or care. But they should. And so should you.

This book is the story of my learning the ways of Silicon Valley from its epicenter, then unlearning them, then finally championing what I've come to see is another way, a better way to build businesses, a better way to do capitalism.

The structure of this book, in three parts, reflects this journey. The first three chapters are about what I've come to see as a very narrow definition of business success, the get-big-fast model dominant in Silicon Valley, that is applicable to very few companies yet applied and emulated broadly. This might seem counterintuitive—to start with the system we don't want to pursue—but it is a necessary exposition. Understanding how and why we've gotten to the point where it's assumed that the best, or de facto, way to do business is scale as fast as possible with massive amounts of investor capital. Before we can undo this system, we must see how that system works.

The middle six chapters are the heart of my transformation—a long, nonlinear, sometimes difficult, often frustrating, but ultimately rewarding journey. By witnessing me unlearn the Silicon Valley way and discover so many examples of companies doing business differently, and thriving, you will begin to find the hope and inspiration I found in those companies. Unlearning twenty years of the Silicon Valley way wasn't always easy, and you will see in some of these stories just how hard it was for me to get out of the mindset, but then also how freeing it was when I gave over to these radically different ideas of how to run a business.

The third and last section gives solid form to all I've learned about another way to build businesses through organizations that are thriving as what I've come to call "Evergreen companies." We will go deep on the practices and principles that make them great, with explicit lessons teased out for how Evergreens outperform in longevity, employee satisfaction, innovation, and long-term, profitable growth, and why it's worth your time to learn and adopt these principles, though many may seem counterintuitive initially. When's the last time someone told you it'd be smart to grow revenues more slowly by turning down customers, or avoid outside capital? You will learn how those strategies work, and why they're worth adopting if you are trying to create something of enduring value.

You'll hear many stories from Evergreen companies. You'll hear about them in the order in which I met them and how each one contributed to helping me shift my understanding of what businesses can be. They help me put together what is now a beautiful mosaic and a powerful framework for growing a profitable, independent company designed to last a hundred years or more in service of the company's Purpose.

Today I am honored to serve nearly three hundred CEOs or presidents of such companies who form the membership of the Tugboat Institute, which I founded to support Evergreen companies and leaders. They are all committed to the Evergreen 7Ps principles of Purpose, Perseverance, People First, Private, Profit, Paced Growth, and Pragmatic Innovation, which you'll hear much more about in the coming pages. Our own research suggests there are more than 100,000 companies in the United States alone that will find deep resonance with these values. It's our goal to bring more and more to light, and to show the world that there is another way to do business, one that will make you feel hope rather than despair; one that will make you happy, not angry; one designed to create value together, not extract it for a few.

In addition, I hope *Another Way* inspires a new generation of Evergreen company founders and the next generation of Evergreen company leaders and owners. The stories here provide Evergreen leaders and owners validation that they are on the right path and can take comfort in continuing to ignore the calls and emails from the legends of investment bankers, venture capital firms, private equity firms, and other alternative asset investors pursuing them for their own financial gain.

A final note on the text. I'm writing this in a style in which in certain cases I'm relaying conversations at critical moments of my journey. These are designed to bring to life those moments, so they're put in conversational form. They are relayed from my memory, sometimes decades after they happened, and are to the best of my recollection good-faith re-creations of the scenarios.

PART ONE

GET BIG FAST

1

The Education of a Silicon Valley VC

To this day, I don't know exactly how I came to be invited into the inner sanctum of Silicon Valley venture capital during the most exciting and transformative period of new business creation in the past fifty years. It was in the fall of 1995, right after I enrolled in the Stanford Graduate School of Business, when a woman who claimed to work for venture capitalist John Doerr at Kleiner Perkins Caulfield & Byers (KPCB) called and said Doerr would like me to meet him at his office on Sand Hill Road.

Kleiner Perkins was then the hottest venture capital firm in Silicon Valley, thanks largely to Doerr. In 1994, he had led its investment in Netscape Communications, which had produced one of the first commercial web browsers, Netscape Navigator. Netscape's IPO was one of the most consequential in history, with Kleiner's $5 million stake rocketing to $400 million, and it was fresh in my mind because it happened just a month before this call.

For a first-year MBA student, Doerr's request to meet with me was like the Pope asking for an audience with a seminarian.

"This isn't real," I thought. "How does John Doerr even know who I am?" I figured one of my new classmates must be pranking me. So I called the main number of Kleiner Perkins and asked to speak with John Doerr's assistant. When the same woman answered, I awkwardly stammered that I just wanted to be sure Mr. Doerr had requested the meeting. She said, "That's right. We talked a moment ago and agreed on a time for you to come here." I was astounded. The invitation was real!

I showed up, nervous and curious, and was ushered into Doerr's office for what was scheduled to be a half-hour meeting, but it soon became clear that we were going to talk much longer. Doerr wanted to hear about my time at the Hewlett-Packard factories in Santa Rosa, California, where I had worked for four summers, starting as a teenager in 1983 and through my early undergraduate engineering years at the University of California, Berkeley.

It was, in fact, my desire to attend a four-year college that had led me to apply for the job at HP. I did not come from a wealthy family. My father had made his career in public administration, in which he had earned a master's degree from the Wharton School of the University of Pennsylvania. He had been county executive of Fairfax County, Virginia, and then county administrator of Sonoma County, whose capital is Santa Rosa. No one gets rich on a public administrator's salary, and I—as well as my older brother and younger sister—had always understood that there were strict limits to our resources. My father had driven home the point when I was in high school. I was at the top of my class and seemed destined for an outstanding college, but he made it clear that he could not afford to pay for my higher education. He suggested I consider attending Santa Rosa Junior College as a first step. Neither I nor my teachers liked that idea. I figured, however, that I could earn the money I would need to pay for a four-year college by working summer jobs. So I wrote to HP, the largest employer in Sonoma County, which admitted me to its summer intern program for aspiring engineers, paying about $6,000 a summer.

The company had three divisions in Santa Rosa, and I wound up working in all three, doing manufacturing and a little bit of engineering. Aside from helping to pay for my education, it had been one of the most important experiences of my life. By the time I was hired, John Young had succeeded Bill Hewlett as CEO, but David Packard was still chairman, and both he and his co-founder were very much a living presence in the company. For eight hours a day starting at 6 a.m., I would sit on a manufacturing line with my coworkers, many of whom had been at HP for fifteen or twenty years. As we soldered resistors and capacitors to circuit boards, or affixed gold components under a microscope, or assembled network analyzer chassis, they would tell me stories. Several times a summer, there would be one about "Bill and Dave."

The story I remember most from the line—there are several versions—was about a manager who had bolted shut some cabinets that contained supplies like soldering irons, PC boards, resistors, and transistors. The idea was for employees to tinker with them in their spare time, but that manager had decided employees were taking too much stuff. The supplies, he said, were for engineers only and he locked them up. As we soldered away, they told me that Dave and Bill had got gotten wind of the manager's action, and one of them showed up with bolt cutters, chopped off the bolts, and said something to the effect of, "That will never happen again. We don't treat people that way. If you're curious enough to want to take home these circuit boards and other things, we encourage you to do it. It doesn't matter what your position is here, whether a manufacturing worker, a secretary, or a janitor."

I just loved that story—the idea that, no matter what your role in this company, you had the opportunity to learn and grow and contribute.

Doerr was interested in my HP experience in part, he said, because his mentor, Tom Perkins, a cofounder of KPCB, had also worked there. He also wanted to hear about my others stops: GM and later president of a small industrial laser manufacturing company called Optical Engineering; consultant at strategy management firm Bain & Company; and a one-year stop as a venture capital (VC) associate at InterWest Partners.

He never told me how my name had initially crossed his radar, but it became clear that he was intent on finding a new associate partner. The success of Netscape had unleashed a torrent of inquiries from entrepreneurs looking for capital, and he needed help. He asked me to work for him full-time the next summer and offered to introduce me to other partners at the firm.

At the time, I had been thinking about several possible careers after B-school. But after my experience at InterWest Partners, being a venture capitalist was not on the list. I told Doerr as much, and that my objective coming out of Stanford was to found and build a great technology company like HP. Toward that end, I wanted to work the next summer at a midsized, fast-growing tech enterprise that was bigger than Optical Engineering so that I could see how it was organized and figure out what it takes to scale such a business.

My disinclination toward VC didn't seem to faze Doerr, who still had me meet a few of Kleiner's other partners, all renowned investors themselves. Ironically, most of them agreed that it didn't make sense for me to work at a venture capital firm the next summer and encouraged me to pursue the kind of summer job I had in mind.

Doerr wasn't deterred. He asked where I hoped to land a summer job. I mentioned Netscape and Cisco Systems, both fast risers. Doerr was on Netscape's board and encouraged me to pick Netscape over Cisco, which he said gave him an excuse and means to stay in touch, and the ability to help me meet Netscape's leaders.

So that's where I wound up. I was assigned to work on two minor projects. One involved contracting with third parties to produce versions of Netscape Navigator in the languages of smaller European countries. In the other project, I helped the product manager of Netscape's e-commerce server. Although Amazon and eBay had been around for a year or more by then, e-commerce was still in its infancy, and not a high priority at Netscape. Within months of the successful IPO, Microsoft had launched a direct assault on Netscape's flagship products with the Internet Explorer 3.0 bundle. That's where the company's competitive focus was: the browser and the web server.

But from my corner of Netscape, and my exposure to the early adopters of the e-commerce server, I was convinced that selling stuff online would become a major deal. I started identifying products people could buy online that would be well-suited for direct shipment. Would that be a positive or negative experience for the consumer? What were the margins on the products? Could the items be shipped at a reasonable cost, and at what frequency should they be shipped? How would you deal with returns? What issues would there be around packaging and delivery? And so on.

When I returned to business school for my second year, I formalized this thinking by developing a matrix of e-commerce possibilities evaluated across a dozen criteria, with superior customer experience always weighted as the most important, followed by shipping costs. Doerr had asked me to keep in touch over the summer and I called a few times. But he had changed executive assistants, and—as far as the new one was concerned—I was just some random Stanford B-school student.

I finally met up with Doerr when he came to speak at Stanford. He spotted me in the packed audience. After his talk, we found each other, and he asked why I hadn't kept in touch.

I said, "John, I've reached out several times, and I'm not getting any reply."

The new assistant was, in fact, the culprit, but Doerr still wanted me at KPCB. So, I began meeting again with him and his partners. He didn't waste any time letting me know his plan to hire a full-time associate partner to work exclusively for him. This individual would be the only non-partner member of a KPCB investment team that included Doerr and his partners Brook Byers, Kevin Compton, Will Hearst, Vinod Khosla, Joe Lacob, Doug Mackenzie, Ted Schlein, and Russ Siegelman. Based on their record of achievement, it is no exaggeration to call them the venture capital dream team of the 1990s.

Months of interviews and discussions followed. The KPCB partners were careful and deliberate, and for stretches I heard nothing, which I didn't mind because I was focused on continuing my research into e-commerce opportunities, enjoying my classmates, and getting the most out of my second-year classes, including one on technology strategy taught by Andrew Grove, one of Doerr's mentors from Intel, and another on entrepreneurial leadership taught by Irv Grousbeck, a hugely successful cable entrepreneur and individual investor.

The partners were undoubtedly considering other candidates as well, although I wasn't aware of them because Doerr always made me feel that I was the most important person around. As my second year was ending, he asked me to start part-time as an associate partner before graduation, and then full-time after graduation, without taking any time off.

It was a tempting offer, because what Kleiner Perkins was doing was so exciting. The internet had sparked a technology revolution, and John Doerr and his team were at the center of it. Doerr had led the firm's investments in Amazon and Netscape. Vinod Khosla, a cofounder of Sun Microsystems, had provided seed capital for the hot new web portal and search engine Excite. Will Hearst was cofounder and CEO of the first high-speed cable internet service, the @Home Network. Kleiner Perkins had—since its founding in 1972—already backed a succession of companies that had ushered in the digital age, including Tandem Computers, Genentech, AOL, Compaq, Intuit, Sun Microsystems, Applied Materials, Citrix, and Electronic Arts, among many others.

I knew that what Doerr was offering me was a chance to be part of history.

But I still had little interest in a career as a venture capitalist. I wanted to be Hewlett, or Packard. I made sure that Doerr understood that my goal was to found and lead a great tech company. I had already been toying with an idea that grew out of the e-commerce work I'd done. I thought drugstores would be a natural for e-commerce. I thought a lot of people would welcome the opportunity to receive their prescriptions, razor blades, cosmetics, dental and first-aid supplies—all that drugstore stuff—on their doorstep on a regular basis. This sounds hardly surprising today, but in 1997 it was a completely novel idea.

Doerr said he had no problem with my intentions but proposed an alternative: Come work for him for two years. Give 99 percent of my effort directly to him, which he said would require tremendous energy and long hours. He framed it as the opportunity of a lifetime because I would be exposed to his incredible network and learn how KPCB built businesses, and some of them would be the next Netscape. Or eBay. Failing to sign up eBay was Doerr's great regret at that time, as he reminded me repeatedly, and he was intent on not letting that happen again. My job would be to make sure we, as a team, didn't miss the next eBay.

If I could do that, he said, a small part of my effort could go to my drugstore e-commerce idea, which KPCB would incubate.

"What?" I said. I couldn't believe it.

He was serious but said I wouldn't be the founder; I'd get a few hours a week to work on it. This was all getting very tempting, and that's when Doerr pushed his offer over the top: Do this, he said, and in two years, he'd help me start my own company and serve on its board.

Doerr was teaching me a powerful lesson. He was getting what he wanted by promising me what I wanted. If I gave him two years of my life, I would learn how KPCB helps build great companies; enjoy an unparalleled perch to understand emerging, major technology developments; see my online drugstore concept brought to life by the best VC in the world; and have Doerr's backing with my own technology startup. He knew that he had me. What else could I possibly ask for?

Actually, there was one other thing: equity. When I finally got the formal offer, the salary was good enough, but there was no carried interest, also known as "the carry," that is, the percentage of investment profits that fund managers receive as compensation.

"John, I'm surprised," I said. "I assumed there would have been a carry portion, even if it was very modest."

This might seem like a strange or bold request, but I had been focused on equity compensation ever since high school when the father of a close friend, who was a successful entrepreneur, explained to me that I would never create any kind of financial freedom for myself and my future family on salary alone. To build wealth, you need equity. I had also learned from the career center at Stanford that other venture capital offers included carried interest, and so it seemed reasonable to expect the same from Kleiner. For me, it was less about the amount the partners might offer than it was about the signal that the partners valued the contribution that I would make by accepting the onerous responsibility of making sure Kleiner Perkins would not miss the next eBay.

My complaint made Doerr sound angry, and he said that perhaps I wasn't a fit for KPCB. He said the company had never given an associate carry.

"OK," I said, deflated, but I'm glad I asked. Doerr came back shortly after and said the partners agreed to give me a small piece of carried interest.

Perhaps it was brazen of me to be negotiating carry with John Doerr, but none of this story probably happens if I hadn't; the small carried interest from that fund that included Amazon, and later a second fund that would include Google, would generate the money I'd need to leave all this behind and go searching for and supporting another way to do business.

I had met my future wife, Lisa Briggs, through a blind dinner date in San Francisco in July 1996, and we'd become engaged the next January. Then that May, I graduated from Stanford business school. After graduation, most of my classmates took time off. I was invited on a very interesting trip to Southeast Asia with my closest B-school friends, but I had to beg off, explaining that Doerr insisted I start immediately.

It felt as if I'd jumped on a treadmill going a hundred miles per hour. In my first week, I traveled with Doerr on a roadshow leading up to the @Home's IPO. Soon after, we headed to Seattle for a visit with Jeff Bezos at Amazon's offices in "SoDo"—south of downtown—a rundown part of the city. I could hear the incredibly loud laugh for which Bezos has become famous as the elevator approached. I couldn't help but laugh and smiled at John. I thought, "I have never heard a leader laugh this way. I can't wait to meet him."

Doerr also handed over to me all the business plans that were coming to him at Kleiner Perkins. He wasn't going to read them anymore. I was. He and I were on the hook for $500 million in profits *per year*, he told me. And don't miss the next eBay, he reminded me.

That was intimidating. I felt a responsibility to spend as much time as I could to make sure that I didn't miss anything. I would often take fifty or sixty business plans with me on a weekend. Most I could dismiss after reading the first three or four pages; a few required a complete read and follow-up questions and meetings.

Reading business plans was just part of the job. I was also attending countless meetings. Aside from those with entrepreneurs trying to raise money, we had Kleiner partners meetings followed by company presentations every Monday, and I went to meetings with John for his portfolio companies, including strategic planning sessions and interviews with people being recruited as executives. Then there was the background research John needed to prepare for his various other meetings every week.

The sheer volume of work was overwhelming. I was living in San Francisco with Lisa, who I married in April 1998. I'd get up early in the morning and drive down to Sand Hill Road where I'd work until late to miss the congestion on Interstate 280. I seldom had dinner because I would just work right through.

There weren't enough hours in the day to do everything Doerr wanted me to do. I told Lisa, "I can't keep up with John. I mean he's up at four in the morning and goes to bed late." We had two-way Motorola pagers so that he could text me and I'd text back.

At 5:00 a.m., I would hear my pager go off. It was always John. "Are you up?"

"I'm up," I replied. Of course, I'm up.

Worse than the grind, though, was the anxiety of the uncertainty. I began to think I didn't know enough to do a good job. I was not familiar with some of the technologies in the business plans I was evaluating. I did not understand, for example, the core technologies in networking gear, which was central to some of the ideas for these new businesses, not to mention a critical aspect of a momentous change happening in the marketplace; fiber optics were replacing old copper networks that strained under even early internet usage. With fiber optic cables being laid, system capacity was doubling every six months. That growth created an opening for a huge variety of new products and tremendous opportunities for entrepreneurs and their backers.

But how did it actually work? Yes, there were people at KPCB who knew, but they were insanely busy themselves. I'm uncomfortable if I don't understand what's going on at a fundamental level, but I didn't have time to learn, so I had to live with the discomfort. Finally, I reached out to an old Stanford business school friend in business development at Cisco, whose business is networking hardware. "I need you to give me a 101 on how networking works at its core," I said. "What's happening down at the movement of the bits?" He said he didn't know. "How can you not know?" I asked, incredulous. "You're buying companies that do this."

"We turn to our technical teams for due diligence on the technology," he said. I felt stuck. I didn't have a technical team to turn to on any of the incredible breadth of technologies that were emerging and being brought to KPCB.

This led to a full crisis of confidence about six months into the job. I felt so inadequate.

I decided I had to come clean with John. On one of our flights, I told him, "John, I really don't know if I can do this job, and I'm concerned about letting you and the partners down. I'm having a hard time saying this to you, but I want you to know that I'm aware of it."

He looked at me and smiled. I remember him telling me, "Dave, you're doing fine. In fact, you're doing better at this point than any associate that's ever worked for me."

A weight lifted. How he said it made it clear he wasn't just being polite. He acknowledged I wasn't there yet, but that my progress was more than acceptable.

"I'm just afraid you think I know more than I do," I confessed to him.

He reminded me what I was working on was new to *everyone*. Many of these technologies, companies, even business models, hadn't existed two years ago. You're doing fine, he told me.

It was a transformative moment for me. I went into the conversation viewing it as a massive risk to even say anything. It could have meant my job if I admitted how overwhelmed I felt. And for Doerr to put what I was doing in perspective and reassure me gave me the confidence I needed. I thought, I'm good. I can do this now. I've always been able to figure things out, and I still can, even on a curve this steep. I felt a surge of confidence that would stay with me for a long time and, truthfully, would help me much later when I set off on my own and had to combat doubts again.

I settled in, read all materials that I could prior to meetings, and listened carefully as the partners and entrepreneurs debated how the future could unfold and they hoped to capture those opportunities. It was different from anything I had experienced before. Doerr and his partners were literally talking about how they wanted to design the future of the world, based on their money, their networks, and their ability to influence perceptions about what should happen. Unlike what I thought of as the typical venture capital firm, they weren't waiting for that next great entrepreneur to walk in the door and show them an opportunity. The Kleiner partners were thinking about the formation of new industries and how to back the people who would be creating them. And I was part of that conversation. With Doerr's encouragement to speak up more and lend my ideas, I became part of this heady enterprise. He gave me the office next to his and we had sliding doors between the offices. He'd often call me in to be part of one meeting or another, and we spoke constantly about what we were seeing and thinking. It was an active learning apprenticeship, and I had the desk next to the master.

To relieve some of the stress I was feeling, Doerr said I should move closer to the office to get rid of my long commutes. He would give us a personal loan to cover the down payment as he said Tom Perkins had done earlier for him and his wife. So Lisa and I moved to a small home on Stanford Avenue in Menlo Park, just minutes away from the office.

It was another thoughtful offer that benefited us both. I was able to be home for dinner with Lisa every night that I wasn't traveling and would get back online for a few more hours each evening like the rest of the partners. It felt so much better and was another timely boost.

I was also still going full steam ahead on e-commerce. I had shared with Doerr the matrix of potential e-commerce startups that I had developed after my summer at Netscape. He asked me to show it to Jeff Bezos. Amazon was publicly perceived to be just a bookstore at the time, but Bezos intended to expand, and Doerr didn't want to start funding potential competitors without giving Bezos a chance to weigh in. I flew to Seattle and met with Bezos, who identified the areas he thought we should focus on. Doerr told me to help each of the KPCB partners do at least one e-commerce investment with Vinod Khosla advocating for a basket of the highest potential, e-commerce startups.

Joe Lacob, for example, is the partner who is now co-owner and CEO of the Golden State Warriors. His principal expertise was in medical technology and life sciences, having led KPCB's investments in numerous companies in that space. I thought there was a potential bonanza in an e-commerce website for used cars and wrote a draft business plan over a Thanksgiving weekend. Lacob—who loves beautiful cars—was the only partner with time and interest to take on the project. Of course, there was already a magazine for the purchase and sale of cars, *Auto Trader*, owned by Cox Automotive in Atlanta. We learned Cox was also thinking about doing a website and was open to partnering. So we did. Autotrader.com turned out to be a great investment for both Kleiner Perkins and Lacob.

By then, I had recruited Jed Smith to be the founder of my online drugstore concept. A friend of my best man, Smith came from an entrepreneurial Massachusetts family, and that caught my attention. When we met, he pitched me on the idea of doing a chain of all-organic corner grocery stores. I pointed out that grocery stores were a tough business, with exceedingly low margins, but what about an online drugstore? Smith loved it, immediately got on board, and went to work developing the concept further and pushing Kleiner to write the necessary checks. As the business began to take shape, Doerr grew more enthusiastic about it, as did Brook Byers, the leader of KPCB's health-care practice, both of whom joined the board.

Doerr suggested that we could accelerate the launch by partnering with Amazon, offering an equity stake in our drugstore company in exchange for access to its rapidly growing consumer base as well as its online retailing expertise, an idea we loved. We all flew to Seattle to see whether Jeff Bezos would sign on.

He was, in fact, interested. We eventually worked out a tentative agreement whereby Amazon would own a third of the company, as would Kleiner Perkins, which would put up $4 million.

It was clear to everyone that the company needed an experienced CEO who could take full advantage of the opportunity we saw. Doerr had his eyes on Peter Neupert, a high-level Microsoft executive who had launched the MSNBC network with NBC and worked directly for Bill Gates. Neupert was happy at Microsoft and initially turned down the opportunity, but after an extended courtship, he came around, provided the Amazon deal closed. He also wanted the company to be based in Seattle, and he wanted to be able to spend time with Bezos. Neupert wound up joining Bezos for several days visiting board members, attending staff meetings, and listening in on conference calls.

Oddly enough, the company didn't yet have a name. We'd been calling it drugstore.com, but that wasn't official. Neupert hired a naming firm to come up with ideas. Finally, at a presentation of possible names, Bezos said, "Drugstore.com is a great name. Why not just use that one?" So Drugstore.com it was.

Another e-commerce investment we came across almost by accident. I had agreed to be a judge in a business plan competition at Stanford in the spring of 1998. I was perusing the submissions one day and came across a proposal for an online wedding registry. It was exactly the sort of e-commerce opportunity that I had been promoting at Kleiner. I sent an email to Jessica Herrin, one of the two MBA students who had submitted the business plan. "Are you serious about this?" I asked.

"You bet I am," came the reply.

"Then pull your entry from the competition and come talk to me," I wrote back.

Herrin later told me she had responded to the email with the same incredulity I had felt when Doerr's assistant called me.

Nevertheless, she and her partner, Jenny Lefcourt, took me up on my offer and eventually launched their wedding registry—Della & James—with Kleiner's backing and Martha Stewart joining its board. Two years later with the dot.com crash, it merged with WeddingChannel.com and took the latter's name.

Networking, moving deals along, horse trading on terms, closing the deal, hiring CEOs and key executives, talking strategy, introducing companies to each other, planning for public offerings. It all sounds like a movie about Silicon Valley, but it really did feel like this. It moved so, so fast and loose. There were more deals, every day.

. . .

John Doerr's relentless energy guaranteed that new initiatives were constantly emerging at Kleiner Perkins, and I inevitably became involved with them. One grew out of his friendship with former vice president Al Gore, who had challenged him to find an entrepreneurial solution to the problem of underperforming inner-city schools.

I had my own perspective on the question, having attended a newly desegregated inner-city elementary school in Richmond, Virginia. At the time, my dad was budget director for the city. I was one of only two white students in my class. It bothered me deeply to learn later that a disproportionate percentage of young boys like the kids I went to school with wound up in jail or dead. I knew that, given the right structure, teachers, and environment, these kids could excel academically. They had been my friends. So, when Doerr asked me to think about the viability of applying the venture capital model of backing entrepreneurs in the education space to transform public education, I eagerly accepted.

As with Drugstore.com and Autotrader, my initial job was to develop a business plan. Lauren Dutton, a close friend from UC Berkeley who had introduced me to Bain & Company, was now at Stanford Graduate School of Business. I knew that she was very interested in improving educational opportunities for disadvantaged kids. I asked her if education entrepreneurs existed, and she told me yes, and they could use all the help they could get, given the daunting task of transforming public education. She introduced me to a student at Stanford named Kim Smith, who had been a founding team member of Teach For America. Smith was smart and passionate about the subject, and readily agreed to help and took the lead in writing the business plan for what we'd begun calling the NewSchools Venture Fund. We presented the plan to a group led by Doerr, Brook Byers, and Ted Mitchell, then dean of the UCLA Graduate School of Education and Information Studies. They loved it.

Next, despite the risk, we put Kim Smith in as CEO with me as an angel on her shoulder. Doerr raised money from a number of wealthy entrepreneurs and venture capitalists in his vast network, while I spent a lot of time with Kim and her team, teaching them how to think about financing in stages to mitigate what I knew would be scarce capital for these companies. This experience as a teacher and mentor reinforced my understanding of the way Kleiner Perkins had supported and financed technology companies prior to the dot-com boom when capital was scarce for them, too.

. . .

By the beginning of 1999, I was nearing the end of my formal commitment to Kleiner Perkins. I reminded Doerr that he had agreed to help me start my own technology company after two years at his side. I asked him if it was time to begin the transition process.

Some partners were urging me to stay, and despite my lack of interest in VC during my Stanford days, I learned that I did greatly enjoy the work. But I was determined not to become an old guy sitting on my porch wondering whether I could have been a great entrepreneur like Dave Hewlett or Bill Packard if only I had tried.

John was supportive. Not only did he remember and stand by our earlier agreement, but he also believed that, in the future, the best venture capitalists would be people who had built and scaled successful companies themselves. The model was changing to faster scale-ups and vastly more capital, earlier. Those who'd been through this tech grinder would understand what it takes to manage an extremely fast-growing venture and could help entrepreneurs on high-trajectory paths. So, he gave me his blessing and said that after I started it and exited, through an IPO, I could come back to KPCB as his partner. I remember he said I could be one of the best VCs of my generation. I was, of course, flattered by his confidence in me.

But as I moved to get up from his desk, I sensed he wasn't finished. And he wasn't. "I just can't let you go right now," I remember him saying.

"Why not?" I asked.

He needed me for another year, he said, and I wasn't completely surprised by his request. I could see how the entrepreneurial environment was heating up even more than it had after Netscape's IPO. Heading into 1999 there was a dot-com boom in progress, and an even greater volume of promising concepts funneling into Doerr. So, I agreed without hesitation to give Doerr another year, knowing he wasn't going to take no for an answer anyway. It was a good choice.

That third year began with two urgent telephone calls in early 1999. One came from Andy Bechtolsheim, a German electrical engineer and another cofounder of Sun Microsystems. The other caller was Ram Shriram, an entrepreneur who had sold his company, Junglee, to Amazon and was now a top executive there. Both had invested their own money in a startup launched a few months earlier by two Stanford engineering students who had produced a new internet search engine that appeared able to deliver better results than others and was adding users rapidly. The founders called their startup Google.

Bechtolsheim and Shriram considered Google an exciting investment opportunity, but they were finding it impossible to get through to John Doerr, which was hardly surprising given the deluge of inquiries he had been receiving. Andy and Ram thought I might be able to deliver a message.

After hearing their take on Google, I was happy to oblige. "I don't think we want to ignore this level of interest from Ram and Andy," I told Doerr, who agreed, and reworked his schedule to make time for calls and meetings with them and with the founders, Larry Page and Sergey Brin.

They wanted a $25 million investment from Kleiner Perkins and Sequoia Capital, with John Doerr and Sequoia's Michael Moritz on the board. They wanted Kleiner to lead the investment. Less clear was how Google was going to generate enough revenue to justify such a hefty investment. Page and Brin were dead set against putting banner advertising on the site, as Yahoo had done. They felt it corrupted the purity of Google's search. Instead, they were going to sell enterprise servers to generate revenues—little hardware boxes that companies would buy to do internal search on their intranet and other databases.

We were skeptical the market for those devices was big enough. But what if Page and Brin changed their minds and became open to selling advertising on Google's home page? A bit of analysis suggested Google could probably be worth half a billion dollars in a couple of years if it did ads, which Doerr thought was good enough.

Support for Google at a partners meeting was lukewarm at best. A variety of search engines—old and new—were vying for primacy at the time and none seemed to have a business model that made sense. Kleiner had invested in Excite, and another partner had looked seriously at Ask Jeeves. No one seemed to view Google as an obvious big winner.

Page and Brin had quietly explored other possible investors, but preferred Kleiner and Sequoia. Unlike the rest of the partners, Doerr was becoming increasingly enthusiastic about making the investment based on their technical excellence and rapid growth rate. After some technical due diligence, Doerr put a term sheet on the table for Page and Brin.

We spent the month of May working out the details of the investment. It was my job to go through the term sheet with Page and Brin—normally a routine process since the document was essentially the same for every deal. But they questioned everything, insisting that I explain what each word meant and why it was necessary. I frankly didn't always have good answers and had to go back to the attorneys and the partners for explanations that were acceptable to the Google founders. By the time we finished, I understood every word and phrase in the term sheet, and so did they. It was another powerful lesson—do not accept blindly "this is just how it's done"—that I would need to call on years later and a lesson that carries forward with me to this day.

The deal closed in June, and soon after, the Google board convened for its first official meeting, which I attended. The first order of business was to identify, select, and hire a recruiter agreeable to the board and founders to start the search for a world-class CEO. Both Kleiner and Sequoia had insisted on this as a condition of making their investments. As the person charged with taking the founders through the terms of the deal, it had been my responsibility to make sure that they had understood and agreed to this.

The founders were, of course, vitally important but—at twenty-five and twenty-six, respectively—Brin and Page were simply too young and inexperienced to professionalize the rapidly growing company. They had demonstrated difficulty retaining deeply experienced executives, which had become a critical factor in the new model in Silicon Valley of scaling companies so quickly.

The board meeting was to be held in a little conference room at Google headquarters on the second floor of a building on University Avenue in Palo Alto. Sergey walked in and announced the new CEO of Google to us. On cue, Larry walked in.

It was my sense that the board was angry, some members red-faced and burning. Heated words were exchanged. Doerr and Sequoia's Moritz demanded their investment back. I was stunned, horrified, and embarrassed in silence—was there more that I should have done? Did I not make this term of the deal clear to them?

Ram Shriram, a board member, ushered the two founders out of the room for a private talk. He then calmly addressed Moritz and Doerr. He offered to buy out all of the Kleiner and Sequoia shares if they really wished to get out, but I didn't think he was encouraging it.

It was an extraordinary offer that would have all but cleaned out his personal wealth on a risk that this search engine would win among many. (Then again, it would have given him a 25 percent share of Google, worth over $500 billion today and making him the richest man in the world.)

His offer and tone seemed to calm the waters. The three of them talked, and the real issue became clear: Page and Brin did not appreciate how important it was to the founders themselves that Google have an experienced leader as CEO. So, the first task was to persuade them, and Doerr took the lead, putting aside the intense frustration he was feeling and his already overscheduled calendar. It was one of the most impressive things I've ever seen a leader do. He told Larry and Sergey he wanted to get everyone back on board with an outside CEO. He suggested they meet with CEOs they admired to get their input.

That summer, they met with a succession of advisers and well-known CEOs, including Jeff Bezos, Scott Cook of Intuit, Bill Campbell (called the "Trillion Dollar Coach" in his biography), and Scott McNealy of Sun Microsystems. All of them delivered the same message to Brin and Page: hire a world-class CEO that you can work with.

It took the rest of the summer, but by Labor Day, Brin and Page were on board.

Google eventually wound up being one of the most successful investments in the history of Kleiner Perkins, along with Amazon, and John Doerr was very kind to give me quite a bit of credit as I was transitioning out of KPCB.

And I had the satisfaction of knowing I had helped ensure that KPCB did not "miss the next eBay," which had been Doerr's critical objective for us from the start.

2

Two Roads Diverged

I had every reason to believe that those three impossibly heady years at Kleiner Perkins Caufield & Byers had given me the best education possible in what it takes to create great businesses. The ones I had helped fund and found were quickly reshaping the world. The proof was in the proverbial pudding: unprecedented fast times from startup to IPOs and mammoth returns.

But that's not all I had learned. I was lucky to have started there at a crucial moment in which this new way of doing business was emerging, but the old way was still very much present, being taught and applied every day. My time there was at the fork between old and new roads.

The old approach to venture capital and company-building was the one that KPCB had used from its founding in 1972. This approach followed what were known as Kleiner's Laws, after Eugene Kleiner, the cofounder, and was based on the premise that starting any business involves risk, of which there are four main types: market, tech, team, and financing. The Kleiner process centered around identifying the risks and then reducing or removing the major ones as early as possible in the life cycle of the company. If there is a fundamental technical problem, for example, you'd want to overcome it before spending millions of dollars on other things that won't matter if the technical problem isn't solved.

The startup would get money in well-defined stages. First, seed capital—up to half a million dollars—for the entrepreneur to do market research, identify key technical resources and maybe some key team members, and produce a business plan. Second, Series A financing to eliminate the most pressing (or white-hot) risks, which might involve building a prototype, getting market feedback, and iterating on the first product. If that went well and feedback was positive, it would open the way to the next financing round—say, $5 million to $10 million to scale the operation and distribution of the product.

Finally, if the company reached $15 million to $25 million in annual revenue and if it had shown consistent profitability for eight quarters, it could go public. An IPO was regarded as the pinnacle of startup success. Kleiner's partners had put hundreds of companies through this careful and deliberate process in its first twenty-five years, including Citrix, Compaq, Tandem Computers, and Genentech.

The new approach emerged, suddenly, after Netscape's explosive IPO on August 9, 1995. Netscape did not follow Kleiner's Laws. Its business model wasn't tested and the market for a commercial internet was largely debated. It had never been profitable. It had released the first version of its flagship product, the Netscape Navigator web browser, only eight months before the IPO. Yet on its first day as a public company, it shocked the business world by almost tripling its opening price of $28 per share before landing at $58.25, giving the startup a valuation of nearly

$3 billion and providing a bonanza for its owners and investors while turning many of its employees into millionaires.

The Netscape IPO was the shot heard 'round the world by would-be tech entrepreneurs, the beginning of the dot-com era. It also upended the forty-year-old playbook for funding startup companies. Unprofitable ventures weren't supposed to be worth billions of dollars, but how could you argue with that share price? Now, a company with a good enough internet story didn't have to show sustained profits before going public. To be sure, other factors would affect its value, including the size of its potential market, the credibility of its leadership team, and their potential to secure market leadership. But whatever those factors might be, it was clear that time required from seed to harvest could be significantly reduced and the exit valuations could be three to ten times (or more) larger than just a year earlier. Kleiner's Laws were no longer the driving framework.

John Doerr dubbed it "get-big-fast," and he was its pioneer and evangelist. The new operational model was accompanied by a change in the way VCs looked at company-building, a new playbook. It had set loose a kind of land rush. If you spotted an opportunity or set of opportunities, you needed to move quickly to put a stake in the ground and secure it as quickly as possible. Just set up camp and figure out the details after you've claimed the space.

Claiming space like this only works, of course, with massive capitalization—that is, with lots and lots of money you could use to hire as many great people as possible and establish a major presence in the market. Whereas the traditional approach emphasized achieving profitability as soon as possible and then funding growth through profits, get-big-fast encouraged the entrepreneur not to worry about profitability. The capital, which at the time was cheap and flowing, would cover the losses and allow everyone to largely ignore financing risk. Venture capitalists wanted the company's entire focus to be on getting so big so fast that it would dominate the space before anyone else could claim it.

Unsurprisingly, there was tension between these two models at Kleiner. The success of the Netscape investment notwithstanding, some partners still preferred the traditional approach. They understood and accepted the need for urgency but not to the point of funding losses in manic pursuit of actual, or sometimes even perceived, market leadership. In their eyes, the get-big-fast approach risked undermining the discipline and foundation-building that would be required for most companies to achieve long-term success. Taken to its illogical extreme, the model could be seen as a way to get big and get out, making the investors and founders rich, with no concern for building anything of meaningful or lasting value. The means would become the end.

Doerr pushed forward with it, and his success with Netscape, Amazon, and Google won him many imitators. Along the way, early-stage investments grew dramatically—from $2 million or $3 million in a Series A when I started at Kleiner to $25 million or even $50 million when I left some thirty-six months later. Investment funds were getting bigger as well. The typical fund size for Kleiner had been $150 million in the early 1990s. Ten years later it was $1 billion.

This transition happened before my eyes. By the time I moved on, get-big-fast had won at Kleiner and was winning everywhere else. Traditionalists remained but were considered fossils. As I was preparing my exit in early 2000, Kevin Compton—a partner I admired greatly—pulled me aside and told me not to forget the model, the old Kleiner model, he and others taught me when I first got there.

I wasn't in a position to take his advice just yet. There was no way I, as a young man riding this wave, could forgo get-big-fast. I was about to experience it myself—as an entrepreneur rather than an investor.

. . .

By April of 2000, I was spending all my time working on my post-KPCB business with my cofounders Joel Jewett, Trae Vassallo, and Danni Emmett. Our plan was to build accessories for Visor, new personal digital assistant (PDA) being produced by Handspring, which was founded by Jeff Hawkins and the same team that had made the wildly popular PalmPilot.

Visor was an attempt to one-up PalmPilot with an expansion port dubbed Springboard that could be used to plug in accessories. We initially called our company Spring Things, but soon changed it to Good Technology.

But what accessory would we build? I was most interested in doing some kind of communications device, inspired by my experience with the two-way Motorola pagers that John Doerr and I had used at Kleiner. They had allowed us to send text messages back and forth (at *any* hour, remember) and build the businesses we did at the pace we did in a way you couldn't before.

As great as the pagers were, though, they had drawbacks. For example, you could, awkwardly, store your calendar and contacts when away from your desk, but changing and updating them was cumbersome and time-consuming. There was no email on them. If we could make syncing wireless and fast, and add a secure email connection, I thought the combination would have a big market for business executives.

But we didn't start there. Instead, we made our first product an MP3 player that snapped in the Visor and played about twenty songs. We didn't build it ourselves; we bought a company that was in the process of creating it, led by a former Apple engineer, Jeff Mock. Handspring loved the idea as one of its accessories. We liked the idea because it was a "bird in the hand" that got us to a product less than a year from incorporation. Very Netscape of us.

So, we bought the company, and Jeff joined us. As we worked to get the now named SoundsGood audioplayer ready for sale, though, I grew uneasy. It became apparent that we would have to charge $250 for the accessory to make any margin because it relied on NAND flash, an expensive new storage tech. That meant our accessory cost as much as the Visor it plugged into. In effect, we would be asking customers to put up $500 to hold and play twenty songs.

Please remember, as you read about some of these technologies from the privileged seat of the future, that while this may seem obvious now, much less was certain then. The iPod wasn't out yet (though it was less than a year away). The demand for digital music was growing but mostly still through pirated downloads through Napster. Likewise, my initial idea for syncing calendars and contacts and mail may sound like a no-brainer, but no one yet knew the inevitability of those ideas. Our bets were as uncertain as bets on AI techs are today. No one was sure where it all was going.

Even as the SoundsGood project proceeded, I hired two Stanford MBAs to spec out the communication device idea hardware and software needs and the potential market size. Rick Osterloh passionately pursued the idea, which to us looked like a better option than the music player. I made the case to the board, but they wanted to stick with the SoundsGood audioplayer. So did Handspring, which wanted it ready in just five months—when a major media campaign for Visor would launch and feature our product. It was a tall order, given we still had to write the syncing code; find a manufacturer partner; source components; come up with branding, labeling, and packaging; produce manuals; and on and on. I was starting to understand what get-big-fast felt like from the other side.

It was a hellish slog, but we made it. SoundsGood was a fully functional MP3 player like nothing else on the market. It won strong reviews and several awards, and we sold very few of them.

I took no pleasure in having my fears confirmed. Much later I learned from Tony Fadell, the so-called "father of the iPod," that he and Steve Jobs were impressed with our product, but Jobs strongly believed that consumers wanted to carry their whole library of songs with them, not just an album. And he knew the expensive flash storage we used was the future but not economically viable yet. So Apple started, in November 2001, with a rugged disk drive and "a thousand songs in your pocket" for $399.

Fortunately, my skunkworks with the Stanford MBAs had deepened my enthusiasm for a communications plug-in to the Visor. I had learned about a Canadian company called Research In Motion (RIM), which built a device that was essentially a pager that could receive email redirected from a desktop. RIM called it a BlackBerry.

Bruce Dunlevie, who was on the board, hadn't forgotten about our earlier conversations. He surprised me by suggesting we run the idea by Eric Hahn, who had been chief technology officer of Netscape and was an email software guru. The idea was good, Eric said, but he wasn't impressed by RIM's software. We agreed that Good Technology, in the heart of Silicon Valley, could do better.

We would need more get-big-fast money to do it, however. With nineteen slides and the SoundsGood audioplayer offering the proof of our capability in hardware and software development,

I raised another $60 million despite the pall cast over the market by the bursting of the dot-com bubble earlier in the year. It was a remarkable feat.

It was also the easy part. The more I contemplated the path ahead, the more daunting it seemed. For openers, we needed to pivot away from Visor to a stand-alone communications device, in part because the radio in our accessory would interfere with the main device. Building a product to stand alone is a much bigger deal than doing an add-on. It meant finding a new manufacturing partner. It meant replacing the MP3 talent on our team with communications and email talent. It meant coming to agreement on new technical battles, like what operating system to use, something our leadership team (including Eric Hahn) was busy fighting over.

I felt overwhelmed by the team's intractable disagreement and worried someone might quit in protest. I was also exhausted—both physically and emotionally—after the three years of long hours at KPCB, followed by this year of bringing the Sounds-Good player to market followed by a full and hard pivot to an end-to-end enterprise data-communication service. But this is how you do it, right? Keep staking ground until you find a huge opportunity that you can exploit, win investor support, and then go go go. The promise of gold at the end of the rainbow—maybe three or five years away—drove a lot of fanatical work behavior, grinding to an IPO, keeping the big payday in sight.

I also felt the pressure of a fresh $60 million in the bank along with John Doerr's expectation that Good Technology would become a market-leading enterprise communications company worth tens of billions of dollars and therefore one of the big winners of his newest fund. I told the board I was contemplating hiring an experienced and strong number two to take some of the operational load off my shoulders. "I'll keep running it as CEO,"

I said, "but I need help. Plus, I have a lot going on in my personal life that I'm trying to keep away from you guys."

In March 2000, right as the dot-com bubble was bursting, my father had been out golfing when a stray, line-drive golf ball came screaming from somewhere and hit him in the left eye, which exploded. The impact destroyed his eye and socket and left his retina hanging in front of his face. With John Doerr's and Brook Byer's help, he was transferred to Stanford Medical Center, the same hospital where my wife, Lisa, was preparing to give birth that week to our first child. I checked on her as she was heading into delivery and then walked to where my dad was undergoing multiple rounds of surgery in hopes of preventing blood clots or permanent skull damage.

Later that year, he was still recovering, slowly. For the first time, I saw despondency set in with him. Lisa, meanwhile, had been taking care of our baby boy, Briggs, virtually alone. "Are you ever coming home?" she had asked me, perhaps even more colorfully than that. "I feel a bit like I'm on my own here." She was right. I had been working six days a week, from early morning to late evening, leaving me very little time to support her.

Seven months on, in November 2000, my mother had a car accident and, at the hospital, was showing unusual neurological symptoms. My brother and I went to see her. Her arms and hands were shaking uncontrollably. Doctors didn't think it was linked to the accident, but they had no idea of the cause. They began a battery of tests, none of which gave them an answer.

I was experiencing more than stress. I felt I had no room to breathe. Everywhere I turned, there was a crisis. Just dealing with my mom and dad would have been enough. Trying to help take care of a newborn and navigating a stock market crash that wiped out my public technology investments and obliterated my savings just as we were building a new Menlo Park house—that would have been enough. Doing a startup that didn't work out after a full-out sprint, then doing another, more complex startup within the startup—that, too, would have been enough. But I was managing them all at the same time and it was grinding me into dust.

With the board's support, I began looking for a number two. I spoke to an old friend, Danny Shader. He had been at Netscape and later started a payments company that I had helped save by arranging a quick acquisition by Amazon. Danny was now looking into doing another startup and had been asking me for ideas. I told him about Good Technology, and I could tell he loved the idea and wanted to bring along John Friend to head engineering. Eric Hahn and I had thought of hiring Friend before, but I hadn't pursued that possibility in earnest because Danny had insisted that he was off limits. Now I could get both of them.

Shader and Friend had just the kind of experience I needed. "Why don't you join me?" I asked. "You can be Good's president."

He couldn't agree to it. He was older than me. (He was forty-one. I was thirty-four.) "If I join a company," I remember him telling me, "I have to be CEO."

"I don't think I'm ready for that," I said.

We agreed to keep talking. Shader knew Bill Campbell having worked for him prior. Coach Campbell was one of John Doerr's best friends and a close mentor to Shader. He sided with Shader and suggested I become executive chairman. It was a relationship that, as CEO of Intuit, he himself had had with Intuit founder Scott Cook. Like almost everyone in Silicon Valley, I had known about their partnership, which was universally deemed to be very successful.

Practically, he said, that meant Shader wouldn't make any major decisions without me and my support, and I'd have fewer tasks day-to-day as Shader would keep the trains running on time.

John Doerr was against a change. Focused as he was on my development and appreciative of my abilities, which he had seen firsthand, he thought it was critical for me to remain CEO. But other members thought a well-rested and more experienced Shader to be a better chief executive of Good Technology.

All this time, I was regularly driving out to Santa Rosa on weekends to check on my mother, who was still going through tests. She was sixty years old and bipolar and had been receiving treatment for that disorder since the 1970s. As the doctors continued to search for the cause of her uncontrollable shaking, they had her try to walk on a treadmill. It was a treadmill operator who finally came up with the diagnosis. "I have seen this before," he said. "She has normal pressure hydrocephalus"—in layman's terms, water on the brain. Treatment followed, and my mother slowly began to recover.

Between dealing with my parents' maladies amid all the challenges of the business, I was stretched thin and increasingly inclined to bring Shader in as CEO. What pushed me over the top was a conversation with Doerr. I had been talking to him about the disagreement over the operating system for our device, and I sought his guidance. He went in a different direction. This moment is etched into my memory. I remember him saying to me, "Go see Michael Dell. Cut a deal to have him make the device and get this thing rolling. Get on a plane and get it done. You are a warrior, right?"

His suggestion caused something to snap in me. Maybe it was the way it was delivered. The presumption. The exhaustion from all the personal and professional issues. Probably all of it. I had just raised $60 million. I got a verbal agreement on a contract with BellSouth for access to its network—a remarkable accomplishment at that time. I needed a head of software development and was refereeing fights over operating systems. Now Doerr was sort of instantly giving me another mountain to climb. He delivered it as practically a done deal, but I knew it was a huge undertaking. "Cutting a deal with Dell" was not just a matter of talking to Michael Dell. It would require Dell buying into our device design, which we hadn't resolved ourselves, and months of negotiation. Not that it was a bad idea, but as I contemplated what doing a deal would require on top of all the other things that had to be done simultaneously, I knew it was too much.

For the first time in my life, I hit my mental limit. I felt a tremendous pressure, what felt like a physical compression on my body and a psychological one on my mind. There was just no way I could lead Good Technology through this ambitious transformation, be there for my wife and a very young son, support both of my ailing parents, and protect my health and well-being. Danny Shader could help. I told him I'd love to have him join Good as CEO while I moved to executive chairman and urged the board to hire him and let him bring along Friend. I even returned a chunk of my founder's shares to make additional stock available to both Shader and Friend while minimizing investor dilution. If they were in, I wanted them really in.

Of course, I was operating on the assumption that Shader and I would work together in the way that John Doerr had laid out for me when he finally agreed to the hiring of Shader. That is, he expected that Danny and I would make all major decisions together. Doerr called it "two-in-a-box." I soon realized, though, shockingly, that Danny did not share that understanding, nor did he share the goal of using Intuit's successful Campbell-Cook model. Danny preferred not to have me around at all. Ninety days after taking over as CEO, he invited me to his apartment. As we sat down, he wasted no time. I remember hearing him say directly, *"I would like you to resign. I will put together a severance package."*

A rage built in me. "Are you crazy?" I said. "I've already let you be CEO, and you agreed to this arrangement. Now, you're asking me to leave?"

He calmly said he thought it was best for everyone.

I bolted and drove straight to KPCB less than a mile away and told John Doerr about the meeting. He called Shader and chewed him out.

I stayed on as executive chairman at John Doerr's insistence. Shader and I were able to develop an acceptable though not particularly good working relationship. He never felt comfortable having a board member and former CEO in executive team meetings. Nevertheless, I tried to be supportive. In fact, despite feeling betrayed, I thought he was doing a good job.

I decided I could contribute best by signing up early marquee customers and effectively became chief salesperson. I was spending most of my time on the road with prospects like Electronic Arts, Citibank, and Walmart, coaxing them to buy our communications device for their executive and management teams, and my enthusiasm for it, tied with the chairman and founder business card, made a difference.

Shader and I kept up a good front, but I felt constant tension between us, and it got worse with time. Shader eventually told me that he wanted me to stop attending management meetings altogether, so it could be his management team.

"I thought it was *our* management team," I said. "I report to you in my sales role, but I do need to have my input heard on major decisions. I'm closing our major customers, including Walmart, and have been effective in understanding their unmet needs and getting them signed up."

He didn't budge, and I felt cornered. He had worn me down with his frequently private, and increasingly public, demeaning comments directed at me, and the obviously superficial public support. Shortly after I was expelled from the meetings, I heard from friends in the company that he told the management team that he was going to fire Walmart, our marquee customer I'd worked so hard to land, because its people were too demanding. With great difficulty and with the board's support, I turned his decision around, knowing it made my plank a lot shorter with Shader. It appeared to me that it made him seethe. I could also see that, if the company eventually failed, I would be the most convenient scapegoat. I decided it would be best for Good and its team for me to get out of Shader's way. At the end of 2002, I resigned as an employee; then I resigned as chairman the following year.

I had been at Good Technology for nearly three years, and it ended so badly.

I was tired and relieved, but also deeply saddened that my relationship with Doerr was damaged by the Good experience. I had killed myself to try to build a highly successful tech company worth a lot of money. I wanted to do it for Doerr and his partners, the other investors, the Good team, and my family.

I was also scared since I didn't know if my reputation had been damaged in the broader community, given Bill Campbell's outsized influence in the tech circles that I ran, and the fact he was close to Doerr and Shader. I wondered if I would ever find a job again. After I left Good, I told my wife maybe we could move to Dallas near her family where I could teach math. She always reassured me that we would be fine regardless of what happened. I wasn't entirely sure.

And it wasn't just about Shader. As a company founder, I discovered how little I liked the get-big-fast process. It may have met the increasing return expectations of investors, but it turned startups into torturous obstacle courses for entrepreneurs, who had to spend an inordinate amount of time and energy on raising the capital required to make the model go; on constant recruiting of key executives; on doubling employee counts annually and then laying people off due to inevitable overhiring; on securing customers and partners with good intentions but typically less than fully formed products and delivery capabilities; on managing board members with different viewpoints and time horizons; on planning, networking, and spinning the story with an eye toward raising new funds; on adapting strategy and tactics to accommodate the newest investors. The experience had cured me of my high school dream to be another Hewlett or Packard. I didn't see how I could do it. If get-big-fast was the formula for building a great technology company in the twenty-first century, I was happy to let someone else do it. I just knew it wasn't for me.

Most of all I hated the toll on my marriage, my family, and my friends. Our second child, a daughter named Rylee, had been born in April 2002. So, we now had two children that Lisa was having to raise on her own because I was never around. If I wasn't traveling around the country, I was consumed by the pressures of working at headquarters with a CEO who I felt was quietly undermining me.

My response had been to dig in harder and put in even more hours. All my attention and energy had been focused on trying to help Good succeed, while proving my worth as an operator beyond just having a vision and building a huge war chest.

My relationship with John Doerr didn't survive Good Technology. Shortly after resigning, I went to see him to talk about what I might do next. I asked about returning to Kleiner, as we'd discussed in the past. He told me it wasn't a good time. He never explained why, although I later learned that most of the partners I'd worked with alongside Doerr either had left or were in the process of leaving: Vinod Khosla, Kevin Compton, Doug Mackenzie, Will Hearst, Joe Lacob, and Russ Siegelman.

Instead, he suggested I jump back in. Do another startup that he could fund. This time, he said, you should run it through the tape. Then, after being a successful public CEO, I could come back to KPCB.

But I had no interest in that. I declined his offer, and we parted ways.

3

To the Valley

As relieved as I was to be free of the overwhelming stress of my three years at Good Technology, the fact that it ended my once-close relationship with Doerr hit me hard. It was the first real failure of my professional life. I was depressed and felt like I was stuck in a deep hole with no way to get out.

You may expect now the epiphany. That out of Good came my realization that there was another way to do business, and I set off on it. But that epiphany wasn't coming yet. I didn't have the luxury of rejecting the current model, never mind thinking about building a new one. As much I was turned off by the experience, I didn't even actively think about whether there was some other model of doing business. I just needed a job.

My Good Technology cofounder Joel Jewitt was the only person there who was privy to the dynamics between Shader and me and talked to me during the low times. While I was still at Good, he had encouraged me to listen to Bill Moyer's six interviews of the influential writer Joseph Campbell in a series called *The Power* *of Myth.** I said I would buy one of his books instead. But Joel insisted I *listen* to the series and hear Campbell's voice.

So I did. Then I listened again. I listened over and over, often stopping to rewind and re-listen to parts carefully, again.

Three of Joseph Campbell's concepts spoke to me. The first was his now-famous description of the hero's journey found in the mythology of all great cultures. George Lucas had adopted it for the original *Star Wars* movie and the arc of Luke Skywalker's story. As Campbell describes it, the hero, called to adventure by a mentor, faces unexpected challenges and temptations, falls into the abyss of despair and near death, has a revelation that leads to a decisive victory, and returns transformed and powerful to help his fellow man. I was in the abyss of despair and found hope in knowing that all the great civilizations recognized this critical step in one's life journey.

Before this, I had never thought of a hero as someone who had to go through a near-death experience first. In the mythology of Silicon Valley, the great entrepreneurs were never failures but warriors. Campbell was exposing the myth, because heroes must have lows, and emerge from them. In the story I told myself about my journey, it gave me a sliver of hope.

The second concept that deeply resonated with me was Campbell's explanation of Friedrich Nietzsche's three metamorphoses of the spirit from *Thus Spoke Zarathustra*. These are the transformations we must experience in life to achieve true freedom of thought and action. In Campbell's words:

> The process starts when you are a child, when you are a
> young person, you are a camel. The camel gets down on its

---

* Joseph Campbell with Bill Moyers, *The Power of Myth* (New York: Anchor, 1991).

knees and says, "Put a load on me." This is obedience. This
is receiving the instruction, the information that society
knows you must have in order to live a competent life.
When the camel is well-loaded, he . . . struggles to his feet
and runs out into the desert where he becomes transformed
into a lion. The heavier the load, the more powerful the
lion. The function of the lion is to kill a dragon, and the
name of the dragon is ThouShalt, and on every scale of the
dragon there is a ThouShalt imprinted. Some of it comes
from 2,000 years, 4,000 years ago. Some of it comes from
yesterday morning's newspaper headline. When the dragon
is killed, the lion is transformed into a child, an innocent
child living out of its own dynamic. Nietzsche uses the
term . . . "a wheel rolling out of its own center." That is what
you become. That is the mature individual.

I viewed myself as a great camel, as high school valedictorian
achieving straight A's since seventh grade. I had been a hardwork-
ing, reliable teenage employee of Hewlett-Packard showing up on
time every morning. I was an honor student in the academically
rigorous mechanical engineering program at Cal while having
a part-time job, being a member of the national champion tae
kwon do team, and serving as an officer in my fraternity house.
I earned an early promotion at Bain & Company and had the
courage to take a job at Optical Engineering hoping to change the
world of manufacturing, while all but one of the Bain partners in
the San Francisco office considered it too risky a career move.
I had put a great load on myself and done what society asked;
I should be a strong camel, not someone giving up and moving to
Dallas. I was feeling weak and wasn't in a place to kill any dragons. But I took strength from Campbell's message and dreamed
that the load that I had chosen to carry throughout my life might

someday reward me as a strong lion able to kill the "ThouShalt" dragon in my life.

The third concept was Campbell's belief that when one pursues their true calling, unexpected doors will open. I was intrigued and probably made hopeful by this, but it didn't seem as though any had opened for me—or maybe one had with Doerr but that was now closed. Then again, it was also possible that I hadn't yet found my true calling and it wasn't time for me to attempt to kill any dragons.

The wisdom of Joseph Campbell led me to look at my whole life in a new and different light. It raised questions in my mind about who I was, where I'd been, and where I was going. In the process, it helped me climb out of the deep hole that I found myself in.

My first order of business was to find a job. I didn't have the luxury of taking my time and going without one. The dot-com crash had wiped out my portfolio of high-flying tech stocks. We had debt, including a huge mortgage on our newly built Menlo Park house, and I was committed to supporting Lisa as a stay-at-home mom.

Where to go next? As I said earlier, doing another get-big-fast technology startup was out of the question; otherwise, I would have accepted Doerr's offer to back me again. While I hadn't gone to KPCB to become a longtime partner, I had loved the experience there, the long hours and weeks notwithstanding. I had put out some feelers to a few early-stage venture firms that had tried to recruit me out of Kleiner in the late 1990s. I knew it wasn't a good time. All the firms were still reeling from the dot-com crash and 9/11. People weren't sure if the venture industry would recover. "It's over," a well-known senior general partner told me. "We'll never do as well as we did in 1998 and '99. It could take us twenty years to make that kind of money again. We may just close the doors."

Word of my status reached Texas Pacific Group (now TPG Capital), a global private equity firm then based in Fort Worth, Texas, with an office in downtown San Francisco. TPG's founders had tried to recruit me in 1999 to start a firm with a $200 million commitment. At the time I told them that I was flattered by the offer but didn't think I was ready to lead a VC firm.

Now, in 2003, one of the founders, Bill Price, called me saying he had heard I was "loose in the socket." Price had been one of my bosses at Bain & Company. He had always been supportive and kind during my early career.

TPG, it turned out, had launched that fund they'd dangled to me in '99, TPG Ventures, with $500 million in commitments. I was surprised I had never heard about it. They still weren't sure they were on the right track. They asked if I would take a look and tell them what I thought.

I wasn't encouraged by what I found. I didn't see anything terribly interesting in its portfolio, and the majority of the $500 million was already invested. They asked me to come and help turn it around.

I agreed. The position would give me a chance to get back into the venture world and see if I could compete without the KPCB brand behind me. I had already seen how the best venture capital firm in the world worked; this job would let me see how one of the best buyout firms in the world worked, too. I did wonder whether an early-stage venture capital firm was compatible with a buyout firm as its parent company, which would obviously have its own values, approaches, risk appetite, and investment philosophies. I had doubts.

The pay was excellent, too, and taking the job lifted that massive burden.

A couple of weeks after I started at TPG Ventures in January 2003, I got lucky when old friend and mentor Dave Strohm of

Greylock Partners connected me to a company named Success-Factors, which was effectively a mash-up of several startups in the same space: performance management software. On its own, each startup had failed. Strohm was hoping together they might be able to make a go.

Strohm had brought in a new CEO for the combined entity, Lars Dalgaard, whom I met and liked. I also liked the market and its model. Most important, SuccessFactors was planning to deliver its products in the form of software as a service (SaaS), a relatively new concept in Silicon Valley back then. Its most noteworthy practitioner was Salesforce.com, a customer relationship management (CRM) startup in San Francisco, founded four years earlier. From my Kleiner experiences, I knew that the planned switch to SaaS would utterly transform the business, from sales and distribution to installation and maintenance.

I thought SuccessFactors was exactly the kind of startup that Kleiner Perkins would have snapped up in a second, but decision makers at TPG didn't buy in. They didn't get SaaS's potential, and they weren't impressed with the company's leadership. I was exasperated. "All you guys see are the red lights," I said. "If I had presented this opportunity to my old partners at Kleiner, it would be green lights all over. Their question would be, 'How much of SuccessFactors can we own?'" We were talking about a $4 million investment for 25 percent of the company—a modest amount for a $500 million fund. A firm like Kleiner would have thought of this as a small risk. A buyout firm like TPG saw it as a much bigger risk.

I didn't back down. I remodeled the financials and got the partners to reluctantly agree to the investment. Later, one of my TPG Ventures partners scolded me. "You need to know that you pushed too hard here," he said. "You have just put enough rope around your neck to hang yourself."

Dalgaard, with Strohm and my encouragement and guidance, would build the firm consistent with the old KPCB playbook of staged, modestly sized financings that valued every dollar invested.

Next, I brought in LinkedIn. The company was looking for $4 million, and we would partner with an old Valley firm called Mayfield to chip in two each. I had spent time with Reid Hoffman, the founder and CEO of LinkedIn, and his half-dozen teammates in his office in Mountain View. Hoffman was clearly very smart and had big ideas. I loved his energy and can-do attitude. I brought him in for an informal conversation with two of my TPG Ventures partners to avoid an embarrassing repeat of my experience with SuccessFactors, when our team wasn't impressed with the CEO.

Once again, TPG partners didn't like Reid or his ideas. When Hoffman walked out, one partner said, "That guy sweats too much. He's going to have a heart attack. He needs medication, not capital. This guy isn't CEO material."

I thought that was ludicrous. Hoffman was a great entrepreneur.

They didn't see the point in building a network of professionals to share introductions and connections and became annoyed with me, again, for pushing. To me it was so low risk, only $2 million for 15 to 20 percent of the company, but they had capitulated on SuccessFactors, so for LinkedIn, they said, "*Not this time.*" I was brought in to lead the group, so I wanted to design the investment approach, comporting with the old pre-Netscape Kleiner playbook. I almost had to because the TPG Ventures fund had very little capital left, and I couldn't just throw money around. But it seemed the pendulum had swung past the old playbook to something too conservative and too risk averse.

I wished it was the other way around. Eventually, SuccessFactors went public and was sold to SAP for $3.4 billion—what I believe was the best investment of TPG Ventures' fund, and one of the best investments, as a multiple of invested capital, in TPG's history.

But LinkedIn went to Microsoft some years later for $26.2 billion. The partner who questioned Hoffman asked me after how much each of us would have made personally if we had made the investment. "Over $100 million each," I told him. Even better, the twin wins of SuccessFactors and LinkedIn would have established TPG Ventures and me as a significant player in the entrepreneurial community and brought more great entrepreneurs to its doors.

I wound up making five investments for TPG Ventures. The one that the partners liked most was a board game company called Cranium, which was also the name of its signature product. The company had annual sales of about $32 million and was growing. Most important, it had a strong brand.

The TPG Ventures partners and TPG founders loved it. "Everybody's wife and kids know what Cranium is," one of them declared. I thought Cranium was interesting, although it was not an opportunity that I could get excited about. I preferred high-risk, high-reward, early-stage companies, especially those like SuccessFactors exploring new software models, like software as a service. Cranium was a board game, as low-tech as a product can be, and already had been in the market, so it was a growth investment. Still, we made the investment and pushed for growth, selling it a few years later to Hasbro, the toy company, for a modest $77.5 million. TPG got its investment back but made little money.

Those three investment decisions gave me the data points I needed to understand what TPG Ventures was, and it wasn't for me. I don't want to be critical of TPG. I still hold the founders in very high regard. We just had a different mindset about investing at that time. That divergence had always been a possibility, as founder Jim Coulter acknowledged early on. He viewed this as an experiment for both of us, noting that I hadn't work in their type of firm before, and they had not worked with someone with my background before.

· · ·

After about a year, I initiated a strategic review process at TPG Ventures. Every partner participated. We landed on a strategy that seemed more compatible with what the TPG founders wanted and played better to its strengths—later-stage growth investing rather than venture capital in the early Kleiner Perkins mold. They had hired a new partner, Bill McGlashan, who was intent on building the growth investment practice. He asked me to co-lead, but I told him I preferred to work on early-stage software investing rather than growth investing.

I should note that during this time, April 2004, Google went public at a value of $23 billion. I was a de minimis shareholder through Kleiner Perkins, but suddenly I had significant paper wealth. It was not partner wealth—I had been only an associate. Yet it was enough that it exceeded the personal net worth goals I had set back in college. A friend referred to such an amount as the "beer and pretzels" wealth I would have had if I'd decided to retire at thirty-eight.

But for me, it created a new freedom to think differently about what to do with my life. In Joseph Campbell's terms, a door had clearly opened.

I thought about starting my own fund. I wondered what I could accomplish if I didn't have other people telling me not to do what I believed I should do. Thanks to Google's IPO, I could—if I chose—walk away from my relatively high-paying job at TPG.

I went so far as to write a business plan for the fund I had in mind, borrowing from the classic venture strategy, Kleiner's Laws, that KPCB had followed for twenty-five years prior to Netscape. I could get involved with primarily software startups early (pre-product and pre-revenue) and identify the business risks, then write additional checks as those risks were eliminated and encourage them to get to profitable growth early given that the cost of software development and maintenance had declined precipitously since the late 1990s. I even came up with a name for this approach. I called it Life Cycle Investing.

I presented the plan to the founders of TPG, in case they were interested. They liked my plan conceptually, but it was not something they wanted to do. My fund would be far too small to show to their large base of limited partners. They suggested I do it independently, and two founders even wrote small checks so I could tell people they were investors and had their blessing. It was kind of them, though we all realized I would need much more, and they made it clear I shouldn't hit up their limited partners to raise the fund.

So, I found investors on my own, the first venture fund raised by a single general partner. I raised $50 million from six notable institutional investors and two dozen individuals in my network. I decided to call my new firm Tugboat Ventures. The metaphor was based on tugboats being small, powerful, and capable guides of much bigger, much more valuable ships, and done without fame or fanfare.

. . .

As I was starting independent fundraising, Jessica Herrin visited me. She was the former business school student whom I had helped secure funding for her gift registry startup, Della & James, back in my early days at Kleiner Perkins.

She was starting another company. This one would sell jewelry and accessories to women through trunk shows and parties in the homes of "ambassadors" who would function as the company's sales force. The business, she said, would be "mission-driven"—the mission being to empower economically the women who signed up as ambassadors and thereby went into business for themselves. She needed money to get started and asked if I'd be willing to contribute some of my personal funds.

"So, what's your exit strategy?" I asked.

"My exit strategy is to be rolled out of my office on a gurney," she said. She had not sought investment from a venture capital fund for this reason. She knew VC eventually would force her to sell the company.

"So, it's a lifestyle business," I said, and maybe I was a bit too condescending.

"It absolutely is *not* a lifestyle business," she said, miffed at the suggestion. "It's going to be a big, international business, and it's going to impact positively the lives of thousands of women entre-preneurs. It will be much larger and more profitable than Della & James ever could have been."

This still sounded like wishful thinking to me. "You know that building a significant consumer products company requires at least $250 million in capital to get to scale," I said, reflecting the shorthand math I'd learned at Kleiner Perkins.

"That's not true," she said and reeled off a list of well-known consumer brands that had never raised *any* venture capital or taken private equity. What mattered, she said, was the time hori-zon for getting to scale. She didn't mind taking twenty years. Venture capitalists insisted on doing it in five to seven years—or less. She had already had that experience, and she didn't want to have it again.

I was still using my VC playbook to navigate the conversation. I asked her if she would like me to introduce her to TPG since my fund wasn't yet formed. "No, no, no," she said. "They'll eventually want me to sell. I don't want to be put in that situation."

"How about my new firm, Tugboat Ventures, once my fund is closed?" I said.

"Dave, it's a venture capital fund," she said, probably exasperated by my not seeing her intentions. "Maybe you can be more patient, but you're still going to need me to sell the company at some point. That's why I want your personal money."

Out of my deep respect for Herrin, I agreed to put in some of my own money. She said my return would be paid out of the company's profits, forever.

Assuming there are any, I thought. I knew I couldn't count on ever getting back the money I'd invested. Meanwhile, I had my own startup to focus on, and that's exactly what I did for the next seven years.

. . .

I formally launched Tugboat Ventures in March 2006 and started investing almost immediately, using my Life Cycle methodology. I was looking for pre-product, pre-revenue startups built around big ideas, which I found the most exciting and thought offered the best opportunity for a super-sized exit that would make up for all the ones that didn't work out. Of course, they also carried the greatest risk, although I did not fully understand at the time exactly how much risk I was taking.

Over two years, I invested in nine startups that met my criteria. In retrospect, I realize that this was a ridiculously small number of companies to have in my first portfolio. Very early-stage funds were generally expected to invest in between fifty and a hundred startups. Nevertheless, I thought I could hit a home run with at least one of them because I had done it before. In addition to identifying SuccessFactors and LinkedIn, I was the founding CEO of Good Technology, which was eventually sold to Motorola for $550 million, and everybody made money. Drugstore .com had also done well and was later acquired by Walgreens for $429 million. I had played a key role in Kleiner's investments in Blue Nile and Autotrader, both successful exits. To be sure, there were also failures, but that was normal. No one expects every investment to pay out. I was just so good at picking winners, I thought, that I didn't need to invest in more than nine companies and would focus my energies on them.

That, I soon discovered, was sheer hubris.

As I was completing my investment in the ninth company, the world economy slid into the Great Recession, accompanied by a major credit crisis, when funding froze up for about a year as the stock market crashed. None of the companies in my portfolio had reached profitability; not one was self-sustaining. I didn't have enough capital in the fund to keep writing checks to all of them. Limited partners were telling general partners not to do capital calls for new or existing investments due to their own default risk. The money my startups needed to survive simply wasn't there. When the dust finally settled, just three of the companies were still in business.

Ironically, I had already raised a second fund by early 2008, just before the market collapse. One of my most influential investors liked what I was doing and wanted to own a larger portion of a new fund.

The general rule was to raise a new fund every three years. Since I'd started in 2006, I had not planned to raise a second fund until 2009, but with existing investors already lining up, I figured I might as well accept what they were offering. In about a month, I received commitments of more than $100 million, and settled on $75 million for the second fund, with the understanding that I wouldn't begin deploying it until the next year. That turned out to be a stroke of good fortune because absolutely no money was being committed to new funds in the spring of 2009, while the commitments I had from early 2008 were still good.

I started making investments from the new fund in the second half of 2009, as the market came back more quickly than anyone expected. I had modified my approach. With the new fund, I made twenty-three investments, some larger, some smaller. I had also decided to serve on the boards of fewer companies and simply be an outside adviser to the others. Yet I still endeavored to stay close to all the entrepreneurs, working directly with them as much as I could.

I can see in hindsight that what I was after, what was pulling me more than anything else, was my desire to work with great entrepreneurs like Bill Hewlett and Dave Packard—founders with high character and high capability. After my get-big-fast experience at Good Technology, I had the epiphany that I wouldn't be a Hewlett or a Packard, but I could find talented software entrepreneurs that I could invest in and support with a founder-friendly approach that minimized the need for large, ongoing funding rounds like we practiced with SuccessFactors. Life Cycle Investing could work, I was telling myself, and anyone who might doubt this was possible could look to history: Microsoft, Google, and Amazon combined raised less than $40 million in equity capital before their IPOs. Combined they're now worth more than $6 trillion.

I was searching for another way to build great, long-lasting companies. I was operating on instinct at the time, but I can see clearly now that I was moving toward that goal.

While I was trying to make Life Cycle Investing happen with Tugboat Ventures, a new class of investors, as well as incubators like Y Combinator, emerged with an approach at odds with mine. The somewhat derogatory, though not altogether inaccurate, terms for their strategy was "spray-and-pray" or "bread-on-the-water." Basically, they wrote a lot of small checks to startups, as many as they could find that sounded good, without doing much if any due diligence, without claiming board seats or doing oversight, without even knowing much about the companies. Worse, they were telling entrepreneurs to reject any investors offering significant help or asking for board seats. That is, they were encouraging entrepreneurs to stay away from investors with any requirements at all, like the firm I was building. That way, their passive approach would reset the terms of the early-stage marketplace, and they'd use uncapped convertible notes (loans that turn into equity) to avoid having to set a price. The theory was that, if just one bet turned out to be wildly successful, you would make all the money you would need to satisfy any financial obligations and aspirations you might have.

Spray-and-pray was all the rage with former senior and mid-level manager employees of Google, Microsoft, Yahoo, Amazon, eBay, and other firms, cashing out their stock options to try their hand at it. They were, in effect, my competitors. They had no venture capital training, but they had capital. They could, with a clean conscience since it was their own money, "just write a check and get out of the way," as they put it. I might write the same check on behalf of Tugboat Ventures, but I felt an obligation to do the due diligence that I had learned at Kleiner and practiced at TPG Ventures, and to actively help the entrepreneurs I'd invested in. I was using other people's money, after all, and I wanted to be close to the founders and know a lot about them and their teams before committing to what could easily become a decade-long relationship. Unlike the spray-and-pray folks, it wasn't enough for me simply to like the entrepreneurs and their ideas after a short meeting, write a check, then move on. I wanted to understand the risks I was taking and be involved in helping to reduce them. The approach took a lot more time per investment than spray-and-pray—arguably a hundred or a thousand times more if you consider the commitment of serving on a board for ten years or more in contrast to just writing a check. And an investment that gave Tugboat Ventures a 15 to 25 percent ownership stake looked very expensive compared to an uncapped, convertible note.

At the same time spray-and-pray took hold, the typical size of an exit was increasing dramatically, though it took me a while to see it. I was used to thinking that a good exit would be half a billion or a billion dollars. Good Technology's exit for $550 million in 2006 had been one of the biggest of that era. If investors owned 10 percent or 15 percent of a company that had a billion-dollar exit, they could make $100 million or $150 million, which might or might not be enough to "return the fund," as we used to say—that is, sufficient to earn back the committed capital that your fund had started out with.

But beginning in the early 2010s, there were more and more exits significantly larger than I'd seen before, leading up to LinkedIn's 2011 IPO market capitalization of $7.8 billion, followed by its sale to Microsoft for $26.2 billion in 2016. That came two years after Facebook acquired WhatsApp for $19 billion. If you had a small $50 million to $75 million fund and owned 3 percent of a company that had a $20 billion exit, you'd make $600 million, and you'd be a hero, returning over ten times the fund on that one investment alone.

In that environment, spray-and-pray investors did particularly well. In fact, it became clear over time that they might be able to make more money for investors than I could with my highly selective, more paced Life Cycle Investing and do it with much less risk and far, far less effort.

I felt wronged by all this. I had had significant training investing in what I thought was the right way and was coming to believe the new ways were leaving out important and valuable functions from the process. There was just no due diligence; in some cases, I was given *hours* to make an investing decision. It was certain I was not seeing some opportunities directly because spray-and-prayers were blocking me out, knowing my process was more hands-on and involved.

It felt like the ground was moving under my feet. The goal posts hadn't moved so much as the sport had changed entirely right in the middle of the game. Spray-and-pray was an existential threat to what I was trying to build.

By 2011—three years after raising the second Tugboat Ventures fund, when it was time to make a plan for raising capital for a third fund—I wondered whether I should modify my investment strategy again and, if so, by how much. While I was pondering what to do, I learned that the firm of my lead investor, who had encouraged me in 2010 to start the fundraising process for a third fund, was having doubts about my approach. There had been a change at the top of the firm, and my sponsor, who was cofounder of the firm, was out. A younger partner told me directly that the partners wanted to see more results. "We don't know if this strategy of yours is working," he said. He pointed to my limited number of investments compared to others making a hundred investments or more, and how others were not serving on boards, and getting into some very interesting companies. The partners he said, were willing to "listen to my plea"—which, given our history going back to KPCB and my close relationship with the former head of the firm, I found insulting. They weren't saying, "*We won't back you.*" Just, "*We're concerned.*"

Frankly, I was concerned, too. I had a growing sense of being entirely out of sync with the times. I voiced my concerns to a mentor of mine, Burt McMurtry, who had been one of the earliest venture capitalists in Silicon Valley and, more recently, chair of the Stanford board of trustees. Maybe I need to make fifty to a hundred investments, I said, like the spray-and-prayers. Maybe I need to be running around to all the gatherings and cocktail parties where people meet entrepreneurs and write small checks to anyone who grabs me. Maybe I don't need to serve on boards, do all this due diligence.

"Is that you?" he asked. Burt had a way of getting right to it.

"No, it's not me," I admitted.

"You can't adopt a strategy you don't believe in," he said.

"But that may be what you have to do to make money in this market," I said.

"Well, I think you should find a way to help entrepreneurs in a manner that's consistent with your values and the kind of relationships you want," he said. "I think you actually want deep, trusting relationships with these entrepreneurs. You don't want to be transactional. You want to know who's on their management team, what their spouse's name is, how they're thinking about the world, and what they are learning. You don't just want names on a long list in your portfolio marked green or red to show which ones are working and which ones aren't. That's more like a stock trader. I think you need to keep thinking about this."

I knew he was right, but the more I thought about it, the less clarity I had about what I should do next, because regardless of what was best for me, it didn't mean anyone else would want to be part of it. Silicon Valley was changing. I could see it in the new guard of entrepreneurs and venture capitalists I was meeting. So many came to me looking for money and just seemed to be trying to figure out what hot buttons they could push to get me to write a first check instead of thinking about what they needed to build a great, enduring company and then finding the right partners to help them do it. I sensed a lack of integrity in their whole enterprise.

Even the entrepreneurs I invested in would often change tunes when they went to raise a future round. Tugboat Ventures couldn't write large follow-on checks given our fund sizes, so we had to bring in new investors, and investors in this period wanted to see only one thing: very high top-line growth—that is, evidence of growth at all costs, the 2010s successor to get-big-fast. They often brought with them ideas from their other successful portfolio companies, or from recent public successes, that they wanted our portfolio company to adopt.

When I objected, they would say, "What's the alternative? We will run out of cash otherwise." If I suggested that the alternative was profitable growth, no one was interested. I was finding it harder and harder to fight against this current.

With historically low interest rates pushing hundreds of billions of dollars into VC every year, capital was overly abundant, and an industrywide growth-at-all-costs approach could absorb practically any investment, even terrible ones. Silicon Valley had moved even further away from the disciplines that made it so successful in its first forty years.

Everything seemed backward to me. Entrepreneurs and their boards were designing their businesses on the fly just to get the next round of venture capital to keep fueling top-line growth. As my friend Dave Strohm said, "Today, companies are being built to raise cash, not to generate cash."

In the old days when capital was scarce, the whole idea was to generate cash early, thus removing financing risk. Now people were doing whatever it took to raise a lot of money from investors in the next round, profits be damned to the point of being a negative

signal to new investors. Entrepreneurs would modify their strategies and financial forecasts based on what they anticipated the
next round of investors wanted to see—not what customers
wanted, not what was best for their employees, not what they
thought would be best for the business long term. Outside cash
was king. It was almost like what I imagine being hooked on a
drug is like. All anyone could do was chase their fix, do whatever
they could to get the next dose.

This was the financial aspect of a broader change to the Valley
I saw take hold at this time. It was becoming a kind of tech Holly-
wood. People were focused on being seen in the right circles, getting media attention. They wanted to be famous. There was an
emerging cult of the CEO. Everyone was celebrating the hot new
entrepreneur who had just raised money or exited at a super-high
valuation. The term "unicorn" hadn't yet been coined by Aileen
Lee, one of my two successors at Kleiner, but the culture of unicorns was emerging. The game wasn't about starting and building great, lasting technology companies anymore. Hot startups
were vehicles to generate wealth, notoriety, and status. People just
wanted to know who the investors were, who was getting rich on
the team.

I was a stranger in a strange land, deeply out of sync with this
Valley.

. . .

While all this was happening, I had started spending more time
in another valley, Sun Valley, Idaho, which was a deeply satisfying
counterpoint to my days in Palo Alto. There, I'd take long walks
with my dog Krypto. I'd bump into people who were happy—a
strange thing—and not only that, happy with lives that didn't re-
volve around the next deal or showing off their wealth. They

were interesting, accomplished people, financially secure, but not defined by their jobs and not playing the status games endemic to Silicon Valley gatherings. When I was in Sun Valley, I noticed my stress drop, and my thinking was clearer. I was energized by the place. It gave me hope.

In retrospect, if I had stuck around Silicon Valley, I don't know what would have happened, but it wouldn't have been what I wanted. I think my time in Sun Valley, those hikes, those people, gave me a perspective and a confidence to fight the current. To stick to my instincts. To build something new and different. This was the epiphany that there is success beyond Silicon Valley, different definitions of it, and different avenues to it.

I started looking for companies that wanted to grow but felt outside of the increasingly toxic Silicon Valley machine, like I did.

PART TWO

A LEARNING JOURNEY

4

Gathering in Sun Valley

When I began my search for people and companies that I could work with that fit a model different from what was emerging in the Valley, I didn't know exactly what I was looking for other than what I'd always looked for: people who were doing business the way that Bill Hewlett and David Packard had done it.

HP had made a deep impression on me from the moment I got my job there in 1983, when I was a sixteen-year-old working on a circuit board hand-soldering line. HP's factories in Santa Rosa were spacious and open, and you could see out the windows all the way to the mountains. People were friendly. Many had worked there for ten or twenty years, and they loved telling me, the rookie, stories about Bill and Dave, and how well they treated people, often becoming emotional as they told the stories. Hewlett and Packard were all about respecting the individual, treating people fairly, encouraging them to explore their creative pursuits. Their stories evoked the glory days of entrepreneurship and growth when Bill and Dave were still leading, developing, and refining the HP Way, and there was a sense of unlimited potential.

The company wasn't without flaws. Looking back now, I can see it had already started its cultural decline. When I got the opportunity to have brief meetings with general managers at HP, I noticed they were good people, but not at all entrepreneurial. In fact, they struck me as bureaucratic. There was a significant gap between what I experienced on the manufacturing lines with the workers and supporting engineers and what I heard from managers at the top.

Still, the experience was overwhelmingly positive and left an indelible mark on a teenager. It became my view of what business was. I believed in HP's people-first management style. I noted how HP was involved in philanthropy. It held family BBQs, supported softball leagues, offered access to hiking trails and nice gym facilities. If employees had kids in college, HP provided them with scholarships and grants.

I had no other experience, so I thought all companies were as good. Reading *In Search of Excellence* by Tom Peters and Robert Waterman when I was a student at UC Berkeley reinforced this notion. I saw businesses as entities doing important things for society and as places where people could go to work and be treated well. It wasn't until I joined Bain & Co. a couple of years later that I realized there were also poorly run companies, with awful leaders. *Those* companies were paying Bain up to a million dollars a month to advise them on strategy, even though many times we could see leadership, not strategy, was their core problem. Since we couldn't fire the leaders who were paying our bills, the best we could do was to develop a strategy that we believed they had a reasonable chance of pulling off.

There were other companies besides HP that, over the years, had opened my eyes to different approaches to business-building than the get-big-fast model. One of them was See's Candies, owned by Berkshire Hathaway. I had been introduced to Berkshire and Warren Buffett all the way back in 1999, right before the dot-com crash, and began reading his annual reports. A friend of mine, Ho Nam, had told me about a guy in Omaha, Nebraska, who had been investing with tremendous success for a long time and did it based on really solid company-building values. That intrigued me. I eventually bought some Berkshire Series B stock in 2001. I really liked what Buffett said, especially the way he talked about people and creating value and not getting caught up in fads. I eventually began attending the annual meeting. Over time, I got a good sense of how he and his partner Charlie Munger thought about investing.

It was strikingly different from what I'd been learning in Silicon Valley. To begin with, their investment horizon was far longer than that of any firm I knew of on the West Coast. In fact, in the case of the private companies they acquired, the investment horizon was often forever. Even if the company wasn't doing well for a stretch, Buffett and Munger were extremely hesitant to sell. If they lost confidence in a public company, they had no qualms about selling their shares, but they had tremendous patience with the management teams of the private companies.

I never saw that kind of time horizon in the Valley, even with those practicing the old, pre-Netscape KPCB model. Even then, an IPO was the endgame. But especially as Doerr's get-big-fast model took hold, everything got manic, hyper. *It has to happen tomorrow, more and more, up and to the right.* Yet here Buffett was saying, effectively, "As far as I'm concerned, I'll own that company for the rest of my life."

People didn't talk that way in Silicon Valley.

Of all Berkshire's companies, See's Candies interested me most because it was the one that completely changed Warren Buffett's investment philosophy, from investing in fair companies at a good price to investing in good companies at a fair price. It was a family business founded in 1921. Berkshire Hathaway bought it in 1972 for $25 million. At the time, it had been doing $30 million in sales with pretax profit of about $4 million across 167 stores. Today See's does more than $500 million in sales with pretax profit of about $100 million.

Along the way, it has received about $7 million in net additional invested capital from Berkshire and has returned, Buffett says, well over $2 billion in cash, which he and Munger have used to buy other companies.

That's almost sixty times a return on investment just from its cash distributions, not taking into consideration the dramatic increase in the value of the company itself. Buffett has called See's "the prototype of a dream business."* But back in 1972, without his partner Charlie Munger's intervention, Warren would have passed on what became a dream business, over a small difference in valuation.

What most impressed and intrigued me was the impact of compounding over an extended period. It had grown from $30 million to over $500 million, while generating over $2 billion in excess cash, and didn't appear to be slowing down. The implications for the See family were obvious. If they had kept all the stock in the company and kept growing stores at the same rate, they—instead of Berkshire Hathaway—could have taken out $2 billion in cash over the next thirty years without selling a share.

Now, a decade after I looked at See's, Jessica Herrin was coming to me with Stella & Dot, her jewelry business that she wanted to build without the Valley machine. It was Jessica who had

---

* Peter Bevelin, *A Few Lessons for Investors and Managers from Warren E. Buffett* (San Francisco: PCA Publishing and Intermountain Books, 2012).

awakened me to the fact that substantial companies didn't have to be built with VC or private equity the way I'd learned at Kleiner and TPG. She had raised $2 million to get started. I chipped in some of it, though less than two other former colleagues at Kleiner Perkins, Doug Mackenzie and Kevin Compton. After investing, we would meet with her every quarter and get the latest news, but I wasn't able stay in such close contact with Jessica for long. The companies in my Tugboat Ventures portfolios demanded all my attention. Between sitting on their boards and working with their executive teams, while simultaneously searching for new investment opportunities, my hands-on approach took up most of my time.

Nevertheless, when I did get occasional updates on her company, I was surprised and impressed by her progress. She got to profitability using just $1.6 million of the $2 million we gave her, and thereafter the company continued to be profitable and self-financing. Soon enough, I learned that Stella & Dot reached annual revenue of $100 million. I had companies in my portfolio that had started with a lot more money and hadn't yet reached that revenue number. Jessica had help, of course, especially from Mike Lohner, an investor and board member with operating experience in a related business. He became chairman of the board and was CEO for a period, during an early, critical pivot in product design, and revamped distribution.

By the time I had reached the crossroads, committed to escaping the Valley's deteriorating culture, and as I struggled to figure out my next move, I was astonished to learn that Stella & Dot's annual sales had reached a nicely profitable $200 million. I resolved to get back in touch with Herrin. The impressive financial results were reason enough to chat, but I was also drawn by Jessica's iconoclasm. She had a view of business success that challenged the prevailing wisdom, and she was *doing it*. She was building something in private that she intended to last forever, and she was doing it in a culture where it was universally understood that going public was the greatest accomplishment a company and its founder could aspire to. I admired both her courage and her bravado. I felt I needed to know exactly what she had done.

When we got to meet, in early 2013, I had her retell me her whole story to make sure that time hadn't played tricks with my memory. I then asked her whether she knew others who were thinking the same way as her: "I mean people who have decided that the whole venture capital, private equity, get-sold-or-go-public path won't fit with what they want to do with their lives and their vision for building a significant, enduring company."

She said, "If you'd asked me that in 2005 or 2006, I would've said nobody, but now I know a few people. They come to me because they've heard about what I'm doing."

At Kleiner Perkins, TPG, and Silicon Valley in general, we had never talked about forever private companies like these. But they seemed to be out there, at least a few. Was I missing something important happening in business? Exactly how big was this phenomenon?

I needed to find out. So I asked everyone in my network the same question: "Do you know anyone who is ambitious to build a meaningful company, one of scale, but who has no interest in raising venture capital or private equity, or being sold or going public?" A lot of people in my VC circles stared at me blankly and said they had no idea what I was talking about, but now and then I'd hear, "Oh, yeah, I know someone you should talk to." That would lead to coffee or a lunch, where I said the same thing I had said to Jessica: tell me everything, in your own words.

For a year, I went on a learning journey. I talked to forty or fifty company owners and CEOs, and several thought leaders. A few were people I already knew, though I had never thought of them in this context—for example, Jed York, CEO of the San Francisco 49ers, whose family had owned the team since 1977. I knew him through my chapter of the Young Presidents' Organization (YPO), a group for CEOs. And when I looked closely, I realized there were quite a few other people in YPO running companies that hadn't raised venture capital or private equity. Many were multigenerational family businesses like Ken LaGrande's Sun Valley Rice. I talked to them, too. Others I spoke to had chosen this model after a bad experience on the venture path.

I was enjoying the conversations. I found them refreshing and insightful. I was on a completely new, and steep, learning curve and that was invigorating for me. These leaders felt very authentic and humble yet accomplished. In most of the conversations, two topics would inevitably arise. The first was *people*—that is, their employees. The leaders would talk about how they treated their people and how important the people were to the business and to them personally. There was a deep appreciation for those relationships. It felt like they had a higher level of consciousness about their relationship to other human beings than most hard-driving Silicon Valley entrepreneurs, who in the climate of the 2010s would initiate a reduction in force after a bad quarter, bad board meeting, or after predictably over-hiring when they raised new funds.

The second was their focus on *purpose*. I kept asking, "Why are you doing this? I mean, why are you trying to build a company that will never be sold, never go public, and will continue beyond your lifetime?"

They would say, "Well, because I've got a really important purpose." Sometimes they'd say "mission," or "vision," or something else. But they were basically explaining why their companies deserved to be on the planet.

I'd spent years meeting with entrepreneurs, and those conversations were almost all about money, never about people or culture. When I asked the entrepreneurs about their goals, the response was always, "I'm going to be big. I'm going to go public. I'm going to make you a ton of money if you back me." It was almost as if they were all reading from a script. When I inquired about what they really wanted personally, they all said, "To lead a really big, market-leading company." That was the dance.

I didn't just talk to founders and CEOs. I told everyone I respected what I was finding in these conversations, to get their input and, honestly, see how they reacted. Did they think this was compelling? What issues did they see? Did they think I was on the right track or needing a course correction? One of those confidantes was Dan Bomze, who was then head of strategy at IDEO, the global design company based in Palo Alto, who told me I was onto something.

I was inspired, and more, I was starting to think I could support these kinds of companies that felt so much more appealing than what I was continuing to see crop up around Palo Alto. Maybe I could help bring them together, share ideas, and bring my best experiences and lessons from Silicon Valley to them.

Bomze thought so, but also knew me well enough to caution me against trying to figure it all out on my own. He suggested I apply some of that design thinking IDEO is so famous for.

He meant that I should invite other people to collaborate on the earliest development of this emerging idea, which was so nascent I didn't even have a name for it. What should I call these companies that could have been built to scale and gone public but instead chose the private path that honored people and purpose?

When I was starting Tugboat Ventures, I had explored the possibility of creating a so-called evergreen venture capital fund, which is a type of perpetual venture capital fund that renews every four years. Unlike VC funds, an evergreen fund has no termination date. It occurred to me that "evergreen" was a good way to describe the companies I was looking for. I talked it over with Craig Dauchy, my general counsel and one of the early pioneers of the still-rare evergreen fund structure. He enthusiastically concurred and gave his full support. So, that's what I was going to do: find and support *Evergreen companies.*

In my next meeting with my mentor Burt McMurtry, I gave my regular update on Tugboat Ventures, but also told him about my learning journey, what I'd seen in these companies I was calling Evergreen companies. He was intrigued. "Tugboat Ventures was interesting," he said, "and I'm glad we tried it. But I think you really need to figure out if there's something here around Evergreen. You should meet with Roberta Katz. She can help you."

He meant Roberta Katz from Netscape. She had been general counsel and one of my managers when I worked there for a summer. Katz was a close friend of Burt's and was now a VP at Stanford.

I met her in Palo Alto, across the street from my old TPG Ventures office. As I told her about the Evergreen companies I had looked at and recounted what their leaders had told me, she lit up. She said, "Like you, I'm discouraged how our values have changed in the Valley, and in business, generally. This idea is very important to our society and a needed one."

I hadn't been looking at the phenomenon from that perspective. "Why do you say that?" I asked.

"Because we've lost track of the importance of human beings coming together to build meaningful companies to change the world," she said.

"Wait a minute," I said. "I want to write down what you just said. That's my purpose statement." I grabbed a piece of paper.

"Really?" she said. "OK."

"Yes, you just captured it. We are going to remind people of the vital importance of human beings coming together to build enduring, private businesses to make a dent in the universe." This immediately became the purpose statement of what I would later come to call Tugboat *Institute* (completely separate from Tugboat Ventures), and it has been Tugboat Institute's purpose statement ever since.

There was another person who played a critical role in the development of the Evergreen company idea—Chris Alden, a cofounder and former CEO of the tech magazine *Red Herring*, whom I'd known and worked with on various ventures since the nineties.

Some months before my lunch with Katz, Alden came to me with an idea for starting a company. This one would provide various business services (for example, PR, sales introductions, planning, back-office work) to venture-backed startups. I told him I didn't think there would be much of a market for such a business, VC firms like Andreessen Horowitz already did that for their investments, and even older firms like Kleiner Perkins had done it quietly for decades. "But let me tell you about some conversations I've been having," I said. I told him about Jessica Herrin and Evergreen companies, all of it, and he got it right away. His parents had started a hotel group that was being run by his younger brother, which sort of fit the bill. "I know exactly what you're talking about," he said. "It's what our family business has always done—financing growth from profits, growing slowly, delivering a quality product, the whole thing. Yeah, I get it. Let me help you."

For the next two years, Chris and I worked together to set up what became Tugboat Institute. I felt we needed an entity distinct from Tugboat Ventures, the venture capital funds. I told Chris that I had in mind an umbrella of services to offer companies on an Evergreen path. At the time, I wasn't sure whether Tugboat

Institute should be part of Tugboat Ventures or a stand-alone entity, nor did I know what services exactly, Tugboat Institute should offer Evergreen companies. One immediate possibility was a convening place for Evergreen leaders. Several of those I'd spoken with during my learning journey were surprised to hear there were other company owners that took a similar approach to business and were curious to meet them. Chris, moreover, had experience staging business gatherings. As for location, I knew the perfect venue, thanks to changes in my personal life.

Right during this learning journey, my wife and children had moved full-time in 2011 to a home we'd purchased in 2009 in Ketchum, Idaho, adjacent to Sun Valley. We made the move because Lisa and I wanted our children to attend the Sun Valley Community School. It stood out for us because of its emphasis on both academic rigor and character development, utilizing the outdoors as well as the classroom. We found Silicon Valley schools far too focused on academic rigor only. The Tugboat Ventures offices remained in Palo Alto, and I continued to work there during the week, commuting to Sun Valley on weekends. This long-distance arrangement had started out as a one-year experiment but had extended into two years and now looked like maybe it would continue longer.

Sun Valley was most famous for its skiing, but it was also the location for high-end conferences hosted often at the Sun Valley Resort. I figured, why couldn't a Tugboat Summit be one of them? I reserved three days, midweek, in October, began extending invitations, and started brainstorming with Chris about what we might put in the program.

Chris observed that we were still missing something important: a framework. We had a good hook, Evergreen companies, but we needed a definition and a framework of what it means to be that; what sets Evergreen companies apart and allows us to own the definition of an Evergreen company. "Maybe we call it the three Cs," Chris offered. "Culture, customers, cash flow."

Good idea. But that didn't quite capture everything I had been learning on my journey and over my life, so I started working on an alternative. That work only reinforced to me just how right Chris was and how important it was to have something. What was the essence of Evergreen companies? What fundamental principles did they all share? What made them different from the hundreds of other companies I'd seen?

I turned the question over in my mind, recalling all those conversations I'd had on my learning journey. I knew two things that would be part of the framework were those two recurring themes I heard in most of my conversations: "People First" and "Purpose."

Maybe we should use Ps, not Cs.

I thought back to my conversations with Jessica Herrin and what had struck me about the path she was taking. Her exit plan, she had said, was to be "rolled out on a gurney." That is, she wanted the company to outlast even her. She was also determined never to sell it or take it public. That gave me two more Ps: "Perseverance" and "Private."

Rate of growth was another key factor. Jessica and most of the CEOs I met on my learning journey had observed that companies backed by venture capital were encouraged and expected to grow as fast as possible—it was built into the model. But all these Evergreen companies, Jessica's and See's Candies, among them, showed you can create tremendous value and generate excess cash if you are willing and able to grow at a moderate rate that doesn't exceed your resources, and if you keep doing it consistently over a long period of time. I could make that "Paced Growth."

Thinking about the pace of growth led me directly to how you finance that. Evergreen companies were growing without outside venture or private equity capital. Maybe they had bank loans. But mostly they had to rely on their own cash flow from operations to finance growth. To generate that cash flow, they needed yet another P: "Profit." The amount of that profit depended on the value customers placed on their products or services, and so profit was also a great measure of a company's success in serving customers. Profits also fund the important activities of reinvesting in the business's growth, rewarding employees with profit sharing, rewarding owners for tying up their capital in the business, strengthening the balance sheet, paying down debt (if any), and financing acquisitions. Steady profits protect a company's independence so that it can continue to achieve its purpose and honor its values.

What was I missing? I wondered how innovation might fit into the picture. I had long been an admirer of Harvard Business School professor Clayton Christensen, the world's foremost authority on innovation, and I was fortunate to connect with him and his team in the months leading up to the Tugboat Summit. Among other things, Christensen had pointed out that Silicon Valley was no longer producing disruptive, market-creating innovations—that is, innovations leading to the development of whole new markets and industries. That helped me realize that Evergreen companies went about innovation in a way starkly different from venture-backed companies, especially the predominant, get-big-fast variety. For an Evergreen company, again, the key factor was time.

As Jeff Bezos of Amazon had observed, "a lot of invention doesn't work. If you're going to invent, it means you're going to experiment, and if you're going to experiment, you're going to fail, and if you're going to fail, you have to think long-term."* That is,

* "Amazon CEO Jeff Bezos Quotes," www.supplychaintoday.com/amazon -ceo-jeff-bezos-quotes/.

you need to give yourself enough time. There is no quick process for creating an innovative product or service; finding an initial market for it and then developing the market while adapting the product or service with customer feedback and experience may take as much as five to ten years before the innovation will start delivering a return on invested capital.

That's much longer than even VCs are willing or able to wait. Evergreen companies, however, by their nature have that kind of time, and they can start small by addressing customer wants and needs as they arise, which they will over and over for an enterprise that intends to carry on for a hundred years or more. This led to the seventh P: "Pragmatic Innovation."

Should there be an eighth P? Were these the right ones and did they make sense? Was the framework correct? Could there be a better one built around, say, Cs instead of Ps?

Frankly, I didn't know, but I thought this felt right and was ready to leap off from here. Chris liked them. They were a good hypothesis, we agreed, and that's exactly how we approached the 7Ps framework—as a hypothesis. For now, we felt good declaring that Evergreen companies followed the Evergreen 7Ps principles:

- Purpose

- Perseverance

- People First

- Private

- Profit

- Paced Growth

- Pragmatic Innovation

We'd need to test this, a lesson from Bain, with other people, especially Evergreen CEOs, before declaring it our official framework. But we didn't want to share it at the fast-approaching Tugboat Summit. I had invited about sixty people to the event, but I had no idea how many would show up or what they would think. It seemed quite possible to me that they'd say afterward, "This was a fun couple of days, but we're not interested in doing it again." And if they had, I would have dropped the idea of the Tugboat Institute and gone back to the drawing board.

Summit aside, I still didn't feel entirely certain that the Evergreen phenomenon was substantial enough to support an organization devoted to promoting the concept. My Silicon Valley training and instincts suggested this might be a small niche. There were moments when I wondered whether I might have made much more of it in my mind than existed in the real world, just because I myself found it so appealing. Sure, many people I'd spoken with had been interested, encouraging, and eager to learn more. But I was also hearing from others who thought I was crazy to be pursuing this.

One of the biggest law firms in Silicon Valley, for example, invited me in to talk to its leaders about the Evergreen company concept. We had a good—and lengthy—conversation. I urged them to create a practice geared toward the needs of these companies. One of the partners told me he got it, and knew some companies like this, and suggested they might look at it more closely.

Then later that evening, I got a call as I drove past Stanford University down El Camino Real. It was another senior partner at this firm whom I hadn't met. "What are you doing, Dave?" he asked. "I heard about your meeting with my partners. Look, you have a good track record in venture capital. You should drop this idea and raise another venture fund. The way we build businesses works for all of us, as it has for you." I never heard from the firm again.

I wasn't upset by the call. I didn't resist criticism like this. I encouraged people to poke any holes in my thinking. In effect I was asking them, "What am I missing?" My friend Pat O'Dea, for example, exposed what looked like a huge hole in my thinking, a fundamental flaw. He was at the time president and CEO of Peet's Coffee & Tea, a (then) public company. As we were hiking one day on Mount Diablo in the East Bay, he said, "Because the companies can't offer stock options, since they're not going to be sold or go public," he said, "that means they can't attract the best talent. Top employees won't work for a company unless it can give them stock options. Without options, how are you going to attract the best people? With a high base salary? I don't think that's enough. How does someone afford a house in Menlo Park if all they have is salary?"

I had no answer for him at the time, and I thought I needed one. Fortunately, I knew a compensation consultant, James Kim, from my time on the board of SuccessFactors. I posed the dilemma to him. How do you attract talent to a company that will never be sold or go public and doesn't offer options?

To my surprise, he told me he was an expert on the topic, as he did most of his work with successful multigenerational family businesses that face this very dilemma. Berkshire Hathaway itself, he said, has the same challenge.

And not to worry, he said. That problem was solved long ago, in the form of long-term incentive compensation. There were several variations of the model available to these companies, and he gave me the names of a few of his clients, an impressive list.

One of Joseph Campbell's unexpected doors had opened for me, and I felt a huge relief. We worked for several months to craft a long-term incentive solution that would align with Evergreen principles. We called it the Evergreen Performance Incentive Program, or EPIP. It was a profit-sharing plan but different from most others in that it incorporated a cost-of-capital component and multiyear payout. James told me that Warren Buffet's incentive plans were similar, reflecting his obsession with return on invested capital and his desire to make sure that managers would operate with an eye not only on profitability but also on the allocation of capital for the long-term health of their companies. The potential rewards of such plans were even greater—and much more certain—than those offered by stock options, which in most startups end up worthless. In addition, James said, companies could also offer employees direct ownership in the business with certain restrictions, although it's typically not necessary.

EPIP gave me the confidence to keep moving forward. And I needed that confidence. I had a tremendous amount riding on the upcoming Tugboat Summit. It was just a few weeks away. Everything I'd been working on for the previous year, not to mention my hopes for the next chapter in my career, depended on its success.

I didn't have enough experience, however, to know what to expect. Our Tugboat Summit was voluntary. I was paying for it, but the attendees would have to take the time off at a hectic time of year, get themselves to Sun Valley, and pay for their own travel and accommodations. How many of the fifty or so CEOs invited would actually come? Twenty? Thirty? Would they enjoy being together? I grew deeply anxious.

I liked our roster of speakers, all of whom had expertise in Evergreen-related topics. Pat O'Dea, for example, could talk about the challenges and disappointments of being CEO of a public company, which had been his childhood dream; Jessica Herrin could tell how and why she had founded Stella & Dot; James Kim could present the EPIP.

Of course, the summit's ultimate success would depend on making these pieces a coherent whole. Fortunately, Chris Alden had experience with logistics, and he did a terrific job, taking care of details that I didn't even know existed.

My anxiety finally began to abate in early October, when we saw that more than fifty people would come, including more than forty CEOs. Chris and I had a fully immersive program for them, starting with an icebreaker on the first afternoon—a scavenger hunt that took them through the best art galleries in Ketchum— followed by two days of short, twenty-minute talks in the morning, outdoor activities in the afternoon, and dinner and entertainment in the evening. The morning format mimicked the annual TED conference, which I had regularly attended and enjoyed.

My fears had been misplaced. From the icebreaker onward, there was a level of energy and camaraderie that exceeded my expectations. People were honest and authentic. They were sharing during the morning sessions and afterward. I saw none of the bravado and insecurity that pervaded Kleiner and TPG gatherings. After dinner, we enjoyed two bottles of proprietary whiskey from the distillery of another Evergreen entrepreneur, George Washington—the founder. The whiskey came courtesy of my college roommate, Rob Shenk, who had become vice president of Washington's Virginia home, Mount Vernon.

Chris and I agreed that something authentic was going on with the attendees. *Wow, this is actually happening*, I kept thinking. Given how the Evergreen company idea was resonating with the attendees, I turned around an important question in my mind: What's next?

I had a couple of options. Three different people had pulled me aside and asked whether there was "a capital piece" to the Evergreen phenomenon, including John Foley, founder and CEO of Peloton. Was I thinking about the capital needs of these companies and how I could help them? I said I wasn't sure. "It would be a shame if you don't figure that out, Dave," said one of them.

"You're an entrepreneur, and the only alternatives out there today are venture capital and private equity, which, by definition, will destroy an Evergreen company. So, you might want to try to get your head around a better capital solution."

Alternatively, I could proceed with the founding of Tugboat Institute, which I had talked about with Chris but hadn't done anything with. My idea would be to build it as a membership organization of Evergreen companies. But how many of them would be interested in belonging to—and supporting—such an entity? And what would Tugboat Institute do? Should we have another gathering? If so, when? Were there services we could provide apart from holding gatherings that Evergreen CEOs would value?

I needed advice. Luckily, I had a whole room full of it. What better advisers than the people that I'd just spent a day and a half with. I resolved to raise the issue with the group the next morning, which was fast approaching. It was going so well, I hardly slept.

5

Launch

The next morning, I asked the attendees: "So what do you think about the last two days? How has this experience been for you?" They responded with lengthy applause.

"Should we do another one of these gatherings in a year or two?" I asked.

Yes, they said. But two years was too long, and the fall wasn't good, so how about next summer in June or July? As glad as I was to hear that attendees were eager to get back together, I was thinking, *Omigod, summer is only eight months away.*

Next, I presented a logo I had commissioned for Tugboat Institute. I had kept it under wraps, unsure if this would pan out. Now I told the group, "With your support, I'm prepared to launch Tugboat Institute. The idea would be to bring you guys together and find other Evergreen companies to join us. Then we would help you connect, share best practices with each other, and celebrate."

The response was a standing ovation. I felt an incredible buzz in the room.

But as soon as the event ended, I knew I'd been given my marching orders to immediately prepare for a second summit, which we'd move to a resort in Carmel-by-the-Sea, California, for the next year as the Sun Valley resort was set to undergo renovations.

The validation I had received from the summit was reinforced a month later when Chris and I traveled to Cary, North Carolina, to see SAS Institute, led by Jim Goodnight. SAS Institute is a $3.2 billion, privately owned software company with 13,000 employees worldwide. Founded in 1979, it has been recognized year after year as one of the best places to work in the world. It is equally famous for its remarkable record of innovation that has allowed it to meet and overcome repeated challenges to its leadership in its core markets. It was pure Evergreen. *Forbes* magazine publisher Rich Karlgaard had described Goodnight to me as "the spiritual heir to Hewlett and Packard."

Our meeting with SAS's leadership team was enlightening— and a little daunting. As committed as I was to serving Evergreen businesses and promoting the Evergreen model of company-building, the conversations reminded me just how much I still did not know about the way that the most successful of them operated and how exactly their practices and approach differed.

After the first summit, we felt much better about the Evergreen 7Ps principles, and we decided to introduce them in a booklet we sent attendees as a memento of the event. I felt momentum building. I felt energized. What at first felt uneasy, a potential personal overreaction to the culture shift in Silicon Valley, now felt like my purpose.

The second Tugboat Institute Summit in June 2014 proved to be another triumph. Some of the Sun Valley attendees dropped out, but new people took their place, so it was about the same size. The energy and excitement were just as intense—maybe more so. Once again, I saw how powerful it was to bring Evergreen entrepreneurs together, many of whom had no idea there were other companies that thought and operated like they did. They needed each other. They wanted inspiration and support. They were eager to share. Their connecting, their shared purpose, their common values provided the impetus for us to keep going.

At the same time, as exciting as this was, I still had responsibilities to the companies I had invested in through the two Tugboat Venture funds. Despite their similar names, Tugboat Ventures and Tugboat Institute were separate efforts. Tugboat Ventures had two early-stage VC funds with ten-year commitments each, and I was on the hook to see these through. This meant I had a bifurcated focus sometimes. There was one foot in Silicon Valley and one in Sun Valley. On the one side, I was trying to manage investments in a capital-efficient style toward a successful sale or IPO that was increasingly out of favor in the Valley with its shift to a high-losses, growth-at-all-costs model. On the other. I was totally energized by these companies that wanted nothing to do with that model.

If anything, my time spent on Tugboat Ventures was reaffirming. It kept bringing me back to Silicon Valley, seeing the dynamics that had consumed the business there, and convincing me I was on the right track with Tugboat Institute. I spent every spare minute searching for Evergreen companies and leaders, and potential new members, and spreading the word far and wide about Evergreen as a route to building great companies.

Three months after the second summit, we decided it was time to formally announce our existence. We put together a 1,700-word statement that explained what the Evergreen movement was, how it got its name, why we had founded Tugboat Institute, and what it would do, including the publication of an *Evergreen Journal* and the concept of a capital resource for Evergreen companies called Tugboat Evergreen. We emphasized that we regarded the Evergreen path as an alternative to, not a replacement of, the venture capital/private equity path, which we recognized might still be best for some entrepreneurs.

On September 19, 2014, we threw a launch party at the Tugboat Ventures offices in Palo Alto, a little celebration of Evergreen companies in the heart of a place that had no patience for such things. Our offices were located in a small neighborhood called Evergreen Park. I took that as good sign.

. . .

It had taken me seven years—from 2005 to 2012—to appreciate what Jessica Herrin had been saying when she first approached me about investing in her startup that became Stella & Dot. Once I did, however, I had tried to learn as much as I could from the Evergreen companies that I was able to identify and meet, and they had already taught me a great deal.

There was Zoho, for example, a multinational software company best known for Zoho Office Suite, a package with multiple cloud-based office applications, ranging from CRM to word-processing. I met its cofounder and CEO, Sridhar Vembu, early in my journey at what was then his US headquarters in Pleasanton, California. (Zoho's current corporate headquarters is in Chennai, India.) He came to our Carmel summit and talked about his early human capital strategy for Zoho, which blew me away. He recruited young people living in Indian villages to serve as the company's code-writing engineers. He identified teenagers who were naturally talented in math and the sciences. Then he would train them remotely. Working for Zoho, they would earn what was by far the highest salary in their villages. Word of the opportunity Zoho offered spread quickly. When I spoke to Vembu, he had about a thousand people writing code in isolated spots all over India.

He told me there wasn't a VC in the world who would've tolerated the risk he was creating with this talent strategy, code written by teenagers in remote villages. The playbook dictated: hire college-educated engineers in Silicon Valley.

But Sridhar was accomplishing two things with this strategy. One, he was building software in a very cost-effective way. Two, he was uplifting many communities in the process. In Zoho, I could pick out several of the Evergreen 7Ps: Purpose, People First, Private, and Pragmatic Innovation.

Or consider Tom Bilyeu, a cofounder and president of Quest Nutrition, known for its protein bars. He started Quest in 2010 with his two former bosses at a software company. Bilyeu recounted to me the moment in 2009 when he realized he needed to leave his software company, where he'd worked his way up to chief marketing officer. The company was ranked number forty-two on Deloitte's Technology Fast 500 list of the fastest-growing technology businesses in North America. "We were making money, winning awards. And I remember standing in this beautiful conference room overlooking the Pacific Ocean, and I turned to my business partners and said, 'I'm completely miserable.'"

He longed to work somewhere where there was a purpose that he believed in. And in saying it, he seemed to allow everyone to feel it. His partners felt the same way, they said. Their mutual passion was health and fitness. Within a year of Bilyeu's epiphany, they had sold the software company and launched Quest Nutrition. Its first product was a protein bar produced in the kitchen of one of the founders. Sales took off. In 2014, *Inc.* magazine recognized Quest as the second-fastest-growing private company in America with $82.6 million revenue, almost two hundred employees, and no outside investors.

Bilyeu told me about one of Quest's first employees, Alex, who had grown up in poverty and ended up in jail for some street crime. He had shown up at Quest and asked Tom's wife, Lisa, to sign a form for his parole officer showing that he had sought a job there, a condition of his parole. Lisa saw something in Alex and introduced him to Tom, who did as well. They hired Alex, and he advanced rapidly. He brought others with similar backgrounds. The only rule for Quest's founders was that hard work equals opportunity. Alex had risen to plant manager. He had done so well that, with the Quest founders' support, he went on to start his own pet food company.

I'd never in my life heard of a venture- or private equity–backed company that would back a firm with this human capital strategy. But Bilyeu and his two partners had found a good strategy. Alex and other talent he brought in were helping the company's meteoric rise.

Quest Nutrition did not turn out to be an Evergreen company. A private equity firm bought a minority secondary stake from the founders in 2015, and in 2019 they sold the company to Simply Good Foods, a publicly owned health supplement company, for $1 billion. Nevertheless, Bilyeu had provided yet another example of the impact that a self-funded company could have when not encumbered by outside investors with their own agendas.

I was about to get an even better lesson in this in November of 2014 when, at Jim Goodnight's invitation, Chris and I took twenty Evergreen CEOs to spend two full days at SAS Institute in North Carolina.

6

Exemplar

SAS Institute sits on nine hundred acres in Cary, North Carolina, land the company owns. Its campus includes a soccer field, a medical center, a swimming pool, cafés and food bars, a basketball court, a hotel, a school, day care, and dozens of other facilities, all dotted with beautiful artwork, and all owned by SAS. The maintenance staff, gardeners, gym staff—they're all SAS employees. SAS pays for day care, and at any given time you'll see fitness classes, yoga classes, basketball games, or other activities underway somewhere in this idyllic setting, all provided by SAS.

Founder and CEO Jim Goodnight insisted from the start that the company own everything—not lease or rent or contract—because he intended SAS to be around forever.

VCs, of course, never want portfolio companies to own land or buildings, the logic being that every penny spent on anything other than the product and funding growth is wasted capital. The sole focus should be the real business—in Goodnight's case, business intelligence software. Why should tech companies be fiddling with real estate and rose bushes?

The venture capitalists' position isn't wrong; it makes sense given their model. They need portfolio companies to grow as fast as possible to get scale and market leadership, thereby allowing their investors to earn the highest returns as soon as possible. For SAS Institute, however, there's no rush. Building value over the long term (almost forty years at the time of our visit) not only results in better returns overall but makes possible a different way of thinking about assets.

Corporate field trips aren't uncommon, but they're usually an afternoon in a conference room, or a day at most. This was different. Jim offered to let us spend two full days at SAS of deep, no-holds-barred learning. We were going to take full advantage of every minute. In planning the visit, we had decided to spend the two days focusing on two of our Evergreen 7Ps principles. Day one we'd look at People First and day two at Pragmatic Innovation— two Ps for which SAS was justly famous for getting right. Goodnight led off with a discussion of his philosophy for maintaining an entrepreneurial spirit, followed by a conversation about why SAS had so consistently ranked at or near the top of the various lists of best workplaces compiled by the Great Place to Work organization. We were joined by the then-CEO of the Great Place to Work organization, China Gorman.

Goodnight and other executives discussed how they thought about compensation, among the contributing factors to its track record. Although SAS pays competitive salaries and provides excellent benefits, it does not offer equity or stock options to employees—an absolute necessity in the world I had come from. Apparently, the employees don't mind. They are fiercely loyal anyway. In an industry where the average annual employee turnover rate is 22 percent, SAS's turnover is 3.3 percent.

The goal of its People First activities, Goodnight explained, is to create an environment that fosters creativity. Thus, for example, he wanted to eliminate any concern that SAS's working parents might have. So, he set up a day-care center on the premises. Parents can drop their kids off on the way to work, then swing by during the day to see how they're doing.

Goodnight also insisted that every employee have a private office with a door that closes. And he once asked employees to reduce their workweek to just thirty-six hours. They didn't have the productivity to make it work, however, and instead were pushing fifty hours a week. So, Goodnight came up with another plan: providing high-end food in the cafés and the restaurant. Though the food was heavily subsidized, employees had to pay $2 for a meal, based on Goodnight's conviction that people must pay something or they will take it for granted and overconsume.

SAS became so well-known for its People First policies that other companies wanting a great workplace began copying what it was doing—literally. Before Google went public, Larry Page and Sergey Brin visited and put together a list of SAS's various practices, which they included in the S-1 form they submitted to the SEC prior to their IPO. Goodnight laughed about it. "They didn't really understand," he told me. "They were just making a checklist. We do what we do because it's what our people want."

One thing they want is to keep everybody employed. Executive Vice President and Chief HR Officer Jenn Mann told us that in the Great Recession, when SAP, Oracle, and every other major software company had massive layoffs of thousands of employees, she conveyed to Goodnight how anxious employees were feeling.

Goodnight, Mann told us, assured her that SAS was not going to let people go even though leadership lacked any future revenue visibility due to the recession.

Mann herself was anxious, having never seen an economy in such peril. But Goodnight, she remembered, said they would be fine and asked her to call an all-hands meeting.

"All hands" included employees in fifty-eight countries, more than ten thousand people altogether. Those outside Cary joined the meeting via video. Mann remembers an inspiring speech in which Goodnight reassured all hands that the company would not lay anyone off. He thanked workers for their loyalty and commitment and asked only two things in exchange: watch every single dollar of spending and do not retrench like competitors are doing. Keep innovating.

Clearly Mann and the entire team were deeply moved. SAS proceeded to have the most profitable year in its history.

As inspired as we all were by our discussions of the People First culture of SAS Institute, it was the next day's exposition of the company's approach to Pragmatic Innovation that I found most enlightening and most shocking, given my education in Silicon Valley, supposedly the most innovative place in the world. Goodnight's philosophy was "digging lots of little holes"—that is, doing many small experiments before committing to a new product or service innovation. Jim Collins had written about something similar in his book *Great by Choice* (coauthored with Morten T. Hansen), which included a chapter titled "Fire Bullets, Then Cannonballs."

My understanding was that Goodnight had originally developed his process of innovation out of necessity. In 1976, he was a professor at North Carolina State University in Raleigh when he cofounded SAS Institute with three other academics. They had no money. To create products that they could sell, they experimented until they came up with something that customers liked enough to pay for its further development. It was a process that, once systematized, could lead to new divisions and new product lines, as SAS had demonstrated repeatedly over the next forty years.

I was very curious to know how it worked in practice. I remember the conversation going something like this.

"I know your concept of digging a lot of little holes," I said. "But there's one part I don't understand, namely, the financing of the innovation. I mean, when do you write the big check?"

"We don't," he said.

I thought he had misunderstood my question. "I must have phrased that incorrectly," I said. "You've dug a little hole; you've done an experiment; you've validated the product; you've received some customer feedback on it, and now the person who's leading the project needs $4 million or $5 million to staff up the team and get some additional infrastructure so that you can build the product for the customer. When do you write that check?"

"That's generally true except for the check part," Goodnight said.

"What do you mean?" I asked.

"We don't write the check," he said.

"So, how do you pay for the next phase of development? Does the division head write a check? Or the general manager? Who gives them the resources they need to pursue that thing?"

"Dave, you're not hearing me," he said. "We don't write checks."

"Then how do you get new products out in the market?" I asked, puzzled.

"It's up to the individuals who are putting forth the ideas," he said. "They have to convince all of the key department heads to give them the necessary resources to work on the project and to do it for free. So instead of getting $4 million or $5 million and hiring a bunch of people, they have to get those heads to believe in the idea, which means they have to negotiate. They have to talk about it, talk about risk reduction, because the department heads are effectively giving part of their budget away to try to develop that new business."

"Well, OK," I said, "let's say they do that exercise and it's going really well, but now you have to write the $25 million or

$50 million check that, in the Valley, the VCs would be writing because they want you to take full advantage of the opportunity and establish the startup as a significant player in the market."

"No, we never write that check," he said, calmly. I'm sure this wasn't the first time a visitor unfamiliar with SAS had been puzzled by the approach. "By the time they get to that point, the project must be able to scale from its own profitability. The borrowed players will be released back to their original functions, and the people doing this thing will start staffing up their core team."

I was confused, and so, I suspected, were the twenty CEOs and four Tugboat staff members sitting with me. How could a company introduce major innovations without financing them? I couldn't believe what I was hearing. I turned to one of the SAS executives, Don Parker. "Don, you're the CFO, right?"

"Yes."

"OK," I said, "it must be my fault for not communicating well. I want you to be really clear because you're the man that owns the treasury. When does SAS write the big checks that actually pay for these innovations?"

Don said, "Dave, we don't write checks. That's just not how we fund innovation in this firm. We fund it out of its own profitable growth by the contribution of the division heads to the idea, and through that process, the ideas get better. There's a negotiation, which leads to improvement. That's why we've never been disrupted by competitors. That's why we continue leading our market."

This doesn't make sense, I thought. I couldn't get my head around it. The SAS team could tell I was vexed. So, one of the senior executives took me through an example, step-by-step, of how he had created a new, successful division, a perfect illustration of the pragmatic part of Pragmatic Innovation.

The example did the trick. I could finally see past my decade in the Valley and realize that this model *could* work. Not only that, it wasn't actually so different from a model I was familiar with—the old Kleiner Perkins model, Kleiner's Laws, that was back-seated, then later blown up, by the Netscape IPO and get-big-fast, and later replaced by growth-at-all-costs. I had spent so long in what I'd call "big-check innovation," under which, if you're a tech startup, you want someone to say, "Yes, we believe in you and your big idea. Here's a big check. Now go build it."

The discipline of the SAS model is what struck me. As those checks in the Valley became ever larger, ever earlier in the process, they forced everyone to be disciplined only about the things that got them to the check. Huge outside investments at that early critical stage of development meant the company was not learning a profit discipline or a customer discipline. SAS had both.

As I looked around, I could see big-check innovation, or at least attempts at innovation, achieving new, unheard-of funding levels. Like WeWork, the office rental startup that crashed. The founder, Adam Neumann, was a master at convincing the investor from SoftBank, Masayoshi Son, to write enormous checks on an idea that didn't warrant such funding. It was a real estate company, but the founder had pitched it as a technology company that was going to change the future of work. If you can convince the money source, then you can fund the "innovation," whether the business is viable or not.

Innovation the way SAS does it must be pragmatic because it is capital-constrained by design, which forces creativity and collaboration. In effect, Goodnight wants all new projects bootstrapped. A person with a good idea finds a few collaborators and customers and takes it from there. Managers must get buy-in on new projects from peers to gain their resources. If the project takes off, they can get more resources, but it must come from customers and peers, and not from outsiders with checkbooks. This constraint-driven approach to innovation, Goodnight believed, fostered the creativity, commitment, and entrepreneurial spirit that continues to thrive at SAS after decades.

The tricky part of his model was knowing when to stop and when to drop old products that weren't profitable anymore. Goodnight noted that the company had more than three hundred products in sixteen different business units. He said SAS had to do a better job of killing off the old ones and training sales representatives on the new ones. And as insistent as he was about having people continue to dig many little holes, he stressed the importance of recognizing when to stop digging those that aren't showing signs of bearing fruit.

Although we had divided our two-day visit into a People First day and a Pragmatic Innovation day, it dawned on me just how closely the two were related. A company can't have one without the other. Pragmatic Innovation involves taking risks. There is a chance, after all, that people will fail in their innovation activities. They will undoubtedly make mistakes along the way. If you don't develop trust with your people, if you don't train them, if you don't empower them, if you don't support them, people simply aren't going to take the risk of digging little holes and attempting to come up with new products, customers, services, processes, or whatever other innovations are needed to grow the company. They're going to play it safe. Playing safe won't earn the company another hundred years of success.

SAS Institute's reliance on Pragmatic Innovation also shed light on the importance of other Ps, notably Paced Growth. In the early years, SAS grew more than 100 percent year-over-year but had no annual growth targets. It still doesn't. Goodnight told us the company only responds to demand. He does, however, watch two key numbers carefully: revenue and head count, to which 80 percent of SAS's expenses are related. "We constantly manage against updated forecasts," he said, "and it's a constant battle to make sure that we're profitable every year, particularly because 28 percent of our revenues comes in December."

Goodnight is also committed to staying Private—another P—although he once flirted with the possibility of doing an IPO. It was in the late 1990s when tech valuations were bubbling. Investment bankers from all over descended on Cary because SAS was one of the largest independent software companies in the world and among the few big ones still privately owned. Goodnight himself owned two-thirds of the stock. The bankers told him it was the perfect time to take SAS public. Goodnight wavered. A lot of his peers told him to do it. Maybe it wouldn't be such a bad idea, he thought. So, he hired a CFO with experience in taking companies public.

The new CFO started the process, writing the S-1 and preparing the organization for compliance with relevant rules and regulations. Along the way, Goodnight—who stood to have more than $10 billion in liquid wealth from the IPO—began to have second thoughts. It was becoming increasingly clear that, as a public company CEO, he would have to make significant changes in the way he ran SAS. He decided to put the IPO to a vote of the employees. They overwhelmingly voted against it, which settled the matter for Goodnight. He realized he didn't really want to go public either. He reasoned that he had plenty of money, a nine-hundred-acre campus with a golf course and hotel, a wonderful workforce, and a nice house, and he was happily married and could travel whenever he wanted. What could he even do with the extra money? He fired the CFO and declared that the company would not go public.

Our visit to SAS Institute was seminal, the first of what we'd come to call "Tugboat Institute Exemplar Visits" for our members.

Whatever doubt I had about Evergreen companies, or the Evergreen 7Ps principles, was rapidly disappearing. The revelation of big-check funding versus constraint-driven funding shook me out of my Valley-bred presumptions of how technology businesses had to be financed. It was a sharp and refreshing reset of how I thought about innovation. It showed me crucial aspects of the Evergreen way of doing business in technology sectors that I had naively assumed were just unavailable to Evergreen companies.

And it had demonstrated the value of taking trips with member CEOs to learn from exemplary Evergreen companies. Here was another valuable experience we could offer members.

But there was still much to be done to make Tugboat Institute sustainable and to grow the concept of Evergreen companies, to help more people see there was another way—a better way—to do business. As soon as I got home, I realized just how much we had to do.

7

Valley of Doubt

Having proven to my satisfaction that the Evergreen company phenomenon was real and important, I was fully committed to building Tugboat Institute as the next, and final, chapter in my career—one that I hoped would make a significant contribution to society.

By the end of 2014, we had completed our first full year of Tugboat Institute activities with two successful summits and the breakthrough concept of visiting quintessential Evergreen companies. With a third summit scheduled for the end of June 2015, we had a chance to build on this foundation and establish Tugboat Institute as a CEO membership organization.

At least, that was what I wanted to do. My partner Chris had a different idea. He was excited by the opportunity he saw for creating an influential magazine and media company that would define a whole new segment of the economy, as *Red Herring* had done with the tech and VC in the nineties. I didn't share his enthusiasm. The internet had toppled the economics of traditional media. I didn't think it was possible any longer to build a media company around a print magazine, and that's what I told Chris.

As a practical matter, moreover, we couldn't follow a strategy I didn't believe in, given that I was paying for everything.

By that point, I had spent close to $1 million to get Tugboat Institute up and running. We explored sponsorships as one way to offset the costs of the summit, but we eventually dropped them at the request of members, who worried about being candid and transparent with sponsors in the room and, in any case, didn't want to be solicited during or after the event. Since sponsors only covered a fifth of costs, it wasn't worth the risk that their presence might undermine the safe, trusted environment we had worked hard to create.

I could justify to myself the money I spent as an investment, just like many I'd made over the years. It was a new venture that I considered important to the world and that I believed would eventually provide attractive, ongoing returns when Tugboat Institute became an invaluable community and resource to these CEOs. So, the first step was to create a trusted community of Evergreen company leaders, and I didn't want price to be a barrier to participation while we were trying to reach a minimum scale.

I had also decided that Tugboat Institute should be a for-profit, self-sustaining enterprise practicing the Evergreen 7Ps principles itself, rather than a nonprofit organization, as some people had suggested. The initial model I had in mind was that of the Advisory Board Company, which had started in 1979 with a mission to "answer any question for any company in any industry."[*] Run for years by my friend Frank Williams, a former colleague at Bain & Company, it had thousands of paying members who were regularly polled to determine their most pressing issues. The organization would then research the issues and report back

---

[*] Advisory Board, "Built on a Foundation of 40 Years of Research," June 28, 2022, www.advisory.com/our-history.

to the members through papers and conferences, among other services. In 2014, the Advisory Board took in more $500 million and was fully profitable.

That seemed a good model for Tugboat Institute. An annual up-front fee would help us know how much money we had to work with during the year. Instead of doing outside research, however, I wanted to curate content from members themselves for the benefit of other members. I loved the idea of tapping into the wisdom of the community and unlocking the best practices, ideas, and tough lessons in business, family, and life for everyone else to understand. In time, we could offer additional high-value products and services.

But what should that annual fee be? One person had voluntarily sent me a check for $5,000 after the first summit with a note saying, "This must have been incredibly expensive." His gesture touched me. He did the same after the second summit, and we asked the other participants to make voluntary payments of $5,000 to help us cover our expenses. Fifteen of them did.

It turned out I needed those donations. I was learning that the first two Tugboat Institute Summits, only eight months apart, cost much more than I had thought they would. Bills kept coming in after the second summit for, among other things, an event organizer and her team, a game consultant, an outdoor stage, the best food and drink you could imagine, a climbing wall, an archery course, and on and on. While it had all helped make for a memorable week together, it came at a price of more than half-a-million dollars.

I was taken aback. I obviously hadn't paid close enough attention to this. We had demonstrated that we were able to design and execute experiences that Evergreen CEOs valued, but now, as we geared up for the third summit, it was clear to me that we had to charge for the affair. I figured we would start with a $5,000 annual membership fee, paid in advance. The fee would cover the Tugboat Institute Summit, our new Tugboat Institute Fall Exemplar Visit like the on-site visit we had just made to SAS Institute, and unique Evergreen-related articles and content. The total we'd raise would be well below breakeven, but I didn't want to move too dramatically away from free, and $5,000 seemed like a fair, safe ask.

Much less clear to me was how we were going to make the next Tugboat Institute Summit happen. We could go back to Sun Valley, but we needed a lot more than a beautiful venue to have a successful experience.

And this time I wouldn't have Chris. In January 2015, with my support, he had left. If we weren't going to be a media company, he realized, he had to find his passion somewhere else. What he had enjoyed most about his summit-related activities, he said, had been the crafting of the icebreaker events—the games and puzzles we used to introduce the attendees to one another. He'd decided he wanted to do it full-time. "I'm going to build a game company," he told me, and he did, using Evergreen principles and hoping to build it in the Evergreen company model. His Palace Games would become famous, especially for its escape rooms, judged to be among the best in the world.

An event organizer was recommended to me who would "run circles around Chris" on events. That was high praise, as I thought Chris's work had been spectacular. Given her experience, expertise, and confidence, I hired her and gave her free rein to organize the event and invite past attendees.

Four months before the summit, I learned that one of the event service providers didn't have a contract with us. That seemed strange. When I asked the organizer about it, she told me she hadn't yet gotten to contracting. "So, how many of our past attendees have committed?" I asked.

"I don't have anyone yet." she said.

This was a disaster, and I didn't know exactly why. Was the membership fee stopping people from signing up? After investigating, my CFO reported the grim news: "The event hasn't been planned. There are no contracts, and nobody is attending. You need to cancel the whole thing."

I was incredulous. Canceling would be the end of Tugboat Institute.

"Maybe," the CFO said, "but it's time to throw in the towel on this event."

"Well, that's not happening," I said.

It wasn't a good situation, but I wasn't going to be defeatist about it. I had launched the SoundsGood player, which was much more complicated than this, in about the same time frame. With Chris gone, my events manager in over her head, and my new CFO unmotivated to save the summit, I had only my long-tenured and loyal executive assistant, Loida Knox, to turn to. I said, "Loida, it looks like you'll have to take charge of the event. I'll focus on signing up members to attend."

We were at a make-or-break point, but there were signs of a brighter future if we could hold on. When we were promoting the Carmel summit, Chris had talked to a writer for *Inc.* magazine, Bo Burlingham (my coauthor for this book), who had expressed interest in writing an article about us. In December 2014, he had come to Palo Alto and interviewed me. During the interview, he had mentioned a book, *The Great Game of Business*, that he had coauthored with Jack Stack, the CEO of a company in Springfield, Missouri. Bo said that what I was describing as Evergreen sounded very similar to Stack's ideas about business. He urged me to read the book, and I did.

He was right. From the first page, I could see that Stack's company, SRC Holdings Corporation, was an Evergreen company. It

had the most People First management program I had ever en-
countered in a manufacturing company.

I called Stack in February, telling him that I wanted to see SRC
up close. Stack told me I'd need two or three days. We set a date.
"You're going to freak out when you come here," he promised.

He wasn't wrong.

8

A Great Game

Even as I was dealing with the teetering summit planning, there was no way I could miss this opportunity to spend two days at a legendary manufacturing company that showed all the hallmarks of an Evergreen 7Ps company.

I flew to Missouri to meet with Stack and experience SRC's culture. He surprised me by greeting me in his pickup truck at the airport, fifty miles from HQ. "Let's get a bite to eat and have a beer," he said.

Stack's strong support for what I was trying to do with Tugboat Institute had a tremendous impact on me. "You're onto something with this Evergreen idea and these 7Ps," he said. "This is an interesting framework." He expressed his disappointment that the Great Game of Business—that is, the management system he and Bo had written about in the book—had not been more widely embraced, and he was hopeful that we could help spread the concept. He seemed as intent on establishing a legacy with another way as I did. "I'm very happy that you've gotten excited about this," he said. "You have a lot of energy, and we need a new generation to move these ideas forward. I am living proof of what you're talking about. I'm one of the people that you're trying to find and identify. I've done this since 1983. If anyone doubts that there are leaders who want to lead this way, I'm here to attest that it's what I've been doing for a long time."

At that moment in the spring of 2015, with the lack of attendees signed up for the third summit, gaining Stack as an ally—a CEO who'd built an over $500 million revenue Evergreen company—and his enthusiastic embrace of our cause was exactly what I needed. It was so helpful to me because I was feeling that Tugboat Institute wasn't out of the woods. I knew there were many skeptics like the senior partner at the law firm who had thought I was crazy to give up my career in venture capital to pursue the Evergreen idea. I felt as though Stack was giving me permission to carry the torch. I shared with him my disappointment in the lack of people signed up at that point for the third summit. I confessed that I had no idea how many Evergreen companies there were. Was it a hundred, or hundreds, or possibly thousands?

With Jack that night, I suddenly felt I had another very powerful ally like Burt McMurtry and Roberta Katz. Until that point, I'd never had a CEO at this level of company scale considering becoming a member.

But here I was, having a great conversation with someone I felt honored and lucky to be sitting with. He was a guy that I admired. After reading Bo's book about SRC, I had thought, "This is an American hero." Now he was saying, *I'm here for you. I'm a case example for you.* That was an incredible gift, but Jack was also offering something deeper. He told me: "I'm in this with you. I will join Tugboat Institute, and I will be part of your Evergreen movement."

I stayed for another day and a half, and Jack took me to three or four divisions, insisting I get as much firsthand experience as possible. One of the sites was SRC Heavy Duty, the original factory that Stack and twelve other managers had purchased in a leveraged buyout from International Harvester Company in 1983. As we walked around the factory, people were working on various parts of the remanufacturing process, which is just the process of breaking down, fixing, reassembling, and shipping back used engines. A guy working a CNC machine looked over and said, "Hi, Jack." So did guys in the welding area and those turning engine parts, or sweeping, or driving forklift trucks. Everybody knew Jack and wanted to say hello.

There was one old-timer who I gathered had been working there for a couple of decades. Jack said to him, "Can I interrupt you for a minute? I'd like you to meet Dave. He's a good friend of mine." The three of us chatted, and then Jack asked if I had any questions for the guy.

"I'd like to know how you think about your job," I said. The guy started talking about standard rates of work, and why the variances were important, how they fit into the bigger picture. I was thinking that Jack must have coached the guy in advance and staged the conversation for my benefit, but Jack insisted he hadn't.

Jack had told me that the company had a goal of putting $100 million in cash on the balance sheet by the end of the decade, so that it would be ready for the next recession, which he expected to start sometime around 2020. "Are people aware of that goal?" I asked.

"For sure," he said. "Every employee understands it as one of our core long-term objectives. That also allows me to feel comfortable handing over the reins because I've put the company in a very solid position."

We stopped again to talk with an employee working in one of the shop-floor departments. Jack nudged me. "I think my friend Dave here would like to know what you think are our most important objectives looking forward a few years," he said.

"Well, there's the $100 million we need to have in reserve," the guy said. "We need it because when we get into the next recession, that's going to create opportunities for us, and we'll need the money to take advantage of them." A cynic would insist it was staged, but Jack reminded me it was not.

I noticed how relaxed he seemed. In fact, everyone seemed relaxed and smiling. It struck me that these people seemed quite happy, which I found a little surprising given the environment. There is nothing relaxed about the remanufacturing process. The used engines that come in are huge, grimy, and caked with dirt and oil. The work is complex with hundreds of parts needing to be disassembled and each part examined and sorted. It's a loud, messy process.

The workspace, in contrast, was flawlessly clean. It reminded me of the Mazda and Honda factories I'd toured in Japan many years before.

After walking through the shop floor, we went to a meeting in the cafeteria, the largest room in the factory. The walls were covered with numbers, noting costs and revenues, week by week. "When do you cover these up?" I asked. "Do all the employees see these numbers?"

"That's the intention," Jack said. "We want them all to see this."

"OK, but what happens when a customer visits?" I asked. "Do you cover them up then?"

"Why would we do that?" he said. "Do you think we're competing on these numbers?"

"Well, it's proprietary information," I said. "You have your margins up there, your inventory, your profits."

"Dave, we don't compete on these numbers," he said. "We compete on the intelligence of our people. It's what they do with the numbers that counts, and they're always changing. These are just our current numbers."

It was as stunning as Goodnight telling me he never wrote the big check. I had never witnessed anything like this. Granted, Jack had written about this in his book. It's one thing to read about it, however, and another to see his system working in real life.

That was especially powerful to me, coming from Silicon Valley. A venture-backed firm would never show financials to employees. Even the thought of it would scare the hell out of them. If they saw that you were losing $2 million a month and had $4 million in cash on your balance sheet, they'd all be looking for new jobs. Instead, they trust that management knows what it's doing. This results in an endless cycle of surprise bad news and layoffs. Most people never see it coming, although the engineers might have an inkling. They tend to smell trouble before anyone else.

The other weekly meeting I went to at SRC was being run by Tim Stack, one of Jack's sons, who was then the general manager of SRC Electrical—one of ten subsidiaries of SRC Holdings. What impressed me in this meeting was Tim's ability to get people talking. He'd call out a name and ask for a number on the cost of goods sold from one person, a number on revenues from another, key overheads from another, and so on. Someone would write it all down on the board. They were building an income statement for the month in real time. They were reporting actuals—in other meetings it would be their projections—and people were cheering at good numbers. Apparently, inventory had ballooned a bit, leading to a three-minute discussion of the problem. "Do we have our arms around that? Do we need to spend more time on it?"

Jack also showed me minigames—that is, the relatively short-term visual-based contests for teams designed to solve problems. For example, if one department is concerned with its inventory levels, the team that runs it might create a visual minigame for a quarter that shows the current inventory levels by painting bricks on the factory wall in bright red. Then, as inventory drops each week, those bricks are repainted gray. Everyone sees the visual progress in the normal course of their workday. When the new target is achieved, the players give themselves some reward—say, a hamburger BBQ. If the team crushes the target, the reward might be a steak dinner. I was impressed by how creative and fun, and widely applicable, the minigames were.

We later went to meet a former employee who had left SRC to start a barbecue restaurant, which led Jack to talk about the variety of "associates" at SRC. "You know, Dave, there are different kinds of people in a company, and you need to acknowledge that," he said. "Not everybody wants to be entrepreneurial or a leader. Basically, we have two types here and we value both immensely. Some love to come in and put in a solid day's work, and that's fine. They are engaged at work, getting it done, and then they go home, eat dinner, and have a nice evening. They've made a significant contribution. But I've got other people who are ambitious for leadership and may someday want to run their own company, or maybe a division of SRC. We have programs for them, too, including encourage their putting in the extra hours to develop themselves. Both types are welcome here." Another revelation: I had never heard anybody talk about making space for two different types of people and celebrating how important they each are to the company.

The barbecue guy was obviously the second type. Jack invested a small amount of his own money in the new business. "Wait a second," I said. "You're giving some of your best people your blessing to go out on their own?" Once again, I was astonished. The man had been a star at SRC. When he felt he had learned enough to start his own company, Jack's response was, "That's terrific." He was celebrating the guy's departure as much as his previous contributions.

In Silicon Valley, the message to key employees couldn't have been more different. There, if you were one of those people and left, you were a traitor. One "coach" was famous for dressing down any executive or key player in a company who was thinking about leaving of their own accord. Usually, the person would meekly back down. This message was the exact opposite of what Jack was saying. For a long time, until recently, especially in the Valley, offer letters included noncompete clauses, legally limiting what you could do next in your career.

Jack introduced me to a young man named Neil in a warehouse filled with scrap metal from the used engines. The company would sell it back into the scrap market when space was needed. But Neil had done an analysis and discovered, as he told Jack, that they could make more money if they timed the release of the scrap into the market, rather than just clear it out as the need arose.

Jack let him run an experiment that led to the formation of an entirely new business unit, Global Recovery Corp., with Neil in charge. I couldn't help but be impressed. A young guy sees a wrinkle in its operations, which he can recognize because he knows the numbers and understands how scrap markets work. He does some research and over time helps build a new subsidiary, creating additional value for SRC Holdings, which is owned 100 percent by the employees through an employee stock ownership plan (ESOP).

It was all fascinating, and I wanted to know more. Stack mentioned that he had done twenty-two joint ventures with large companies, which SRC did to keep the ESOP well-funded. SRC was generally low margin, Jack explained, but high inventory turns meant it generated lots of cash. "Even with that, we need to prepare for periods where the number of retirees cashing out their ESOP shares would exceed our operational cash flow. These joint ventures with large companies are one of the ways we figured out to generate cash beyond just our core businesses' operations."

In the JVs, the big companies put up the money; SRC puts up the team, the know-how, and the systems. The contracts include a predefined price and milestones at which SRC can sell back its half of the JV to the partner.

JVs obviated the need to count on a bank or outside investors to meet its long-term obligations to departing employees. Stack had built in the means to get the cash the company would need to take care of them. It struck me as an unusually clever way to protect the company's independence.

There was still another revelation that had particular significance for Evergreen companies. I had long been brainwashed to believe that most growth companies needed outside capital—equity and/or debt, to grow. "No, that's not right," Stack said. "There's a natural growth rate in business. It depends on your business model and how well you manage your cash flow. If you look at your margins, if you look at your inventory, if you look at your payables and your receivables, you see there is literally a cash cycle, and that cash cycle determines how much cash you can generate in a period, which tells you how much you can reinvest in the business for growth without outstripping your financial resources. For example, if you have 3 percent PBT [profit before tax] on $15 million in sales and you turn your inventory thirty times per year, that gives you more than $1 million per year you can use to grow without taking on outside debt or capital as long as you maintain the same inventory turnover rate and margin."

In my entire experience at Stanford business school, Kleiner Perkins, and TPG, nobody had ever mentioned anything like what Stack was telling me. I was dumbfounded. "What are you talking about?" I asked him. "What'd you just do?"

He said, "Say that I've got a 3 percent net margin, and our inventory turns thirty times per year. I'm assuming we have thirty days to pay our suppliers and customers are paying in thirty days." It was like he was talking Greek. He could tell I didn't understand his formula, and so he said, "I'll teach you, Dave." For Jack, it was second nature, but I couldn't even process what he'd just said. I had no familiarity with organic, self-funded growth rates.

For my whole career, growth rate was tied to availability of outside capital. That's just how it was. In Silicon Valley, your company exists because of early outside capital and grows as fast as the amount of capital you can convince investors and bankers to give you—for better or worse. WeWork was a case in point. It grew incredibly fast while losing tons of money, but only because outside capital, SoftBank, was dumping billions of dollars into it. I'm sure Adam Neumann, founder and CEO of WeWork, had no concept of self-funded growth rates.

This was another mind-bending idea for me. I subsequently did some research and discovered an article in *Harvard Business Review* on what the authors called the "self-financeable growth rate (SFG)" with instructions on how to calculate it.* It is a concept, I believe, that every entrepreneur should know, and yet few did. I was adding to the arsenal of ideas that could help companies find another way, to help them become Evergreen companies.

I left Springfield reenergized and ready to tackle the problems I still had back in Palo Alto prepping for the summit. My experience had fully validated what I had read of Stack and others in *The Great Game of Business*. Beyond the wisdom of the book, I deeply appreciated what a great company Stack and his colleagues had built. They had done it, moreover, with a low-margin business

---

* Neil C. Churchill and John W. Mullins, "How Fast Can Your Company Afford to Grow?" *Harvard Business Review*, May 2001, 135–143.

that not a single person in Silicon Valley would have given a second look. Even back in 1983, before get-big-fast, and for a decade or more afterward, a venture capitalist would have looked at SRC and said, "Shut that thing down." But because SRC was so well managed—and because its people were able to turn their inventory so quickly—they had built a fabulously successful company with a great culture that was a pillar of the Springfield community. This way of doing business really works, if you can escape the built-in biases you come up with in business, as I was doing.

9

Breakthrough

I returned to Tugboat headquarters energized by Stack and SRC. This calling I'd followed was the right one. We *had* to pull off the next summit even if we only had a few months to do it. Loida was working on the logistics. I got down to recruiting attendees.

We had a base of members, the sixteen people who had voluntarily paid their $5,000 fees after the second summit, plus one more, SRC. Add six to eight speakers and some guests, that still added up to just twenty-five or thirty people. We needed at least twice that number to match the attendance of the first two summits, and I wanted even more than that. Partly I wanted the current members to see progress. But also I wanted the Evergreen concept to grow, for more and more leaders and companies to see there was another way to do business. I felt I had to do everything in my power to ensure that nobody would sense regression. I got on the phone.

Somehow over the next three months Loida and I managed to pull it off. We kept the same overall design of the program—twenty-minute TED-like talks in the morning, outdoor recreation in the afternoon, dinner events at beautiful locations in the hills and glades of Sun Valley. Through Loida's heroic efforts, the conference came off without a hitch with comparable quality to the previous ones and at lower cost.

We got more participants than we'd had at the first two. An additional thirty-five company leaders signed up for Tugboat Institute, bringing the total number of members in attendance to fifty-two. (They were all CEOs, presidents, and executive chairpersons—a condition of membership.) With the guests and outside speakers, we had about eighty attendees altogether and a solid program with talks by, among others, Jack Stack, Zingerman's cofounder Paul Saginaw, and Robert Levering, cofounder and director of the Great Place to Work Institute.

Immediately after, I turned back to my search for new members. I had high hopes that the upcoming article about us in *Inc.* magazine would give us a major boost. I knew that Tim Brown and David Kelley, my friends at the Palo Alto design company IDEO, had had an article written about them in *Businessweek* years before, and they told me they had used it for a *decade* to gain customers and develop a national reputation. I wanted the same kind of lift.

Sure enough, the *Inc.* article appeared under the title "Built to Last (and Last . . . and Last)." Tugboat Institute was the principal focus, with a sidebar on the 7Ps. I loved the article, and so did friends and colleagues who read it. I waited for queries from *Inc.* readers to start rolling in.

We didn't receive a single new query.

The silence surprised me. Wasn't anyone in the *Inc.* audience curious to learn more? Again, doubts rushed in that for months had taken a back seat to the excitement I felt after visiting SRC. I had to ask myself, again, if I'd exaggerated the appeal of the Evergreen company idea in my mind and was blinded by a few great examples. Back then I was still working out of Silicon Valley and thus surrounded by people who were either uninterested in or skeptical of the whole Evergreen company phenomenon. I noticed when I was out in the field, or at our events away from the Valley, I felt much more conviction. In our Palo Alto offices, I was a Niners fan in the Cowboys stadium.

I fought the doubt as best I could and I looked forward to our next exemplar visit—this one to the McChrystal Group in Alexandria, Virginia.

I had met retired General Stanley McChrystal through his wife, Annie, at a conference in 2014. I was explaining Evergreen companies and Tugboat Institute to her when she grabbed her husband and insisted that he listen to my story.

Upon his retirement from the army, McChrystal had turned to teaching the extraordinarily effective leadership principles he had developed while directing the successful turnaround of the US war efforts in Iraq and Afghanistan. He was now teaching a course at Yale University and had begun writing books. He had also cofounded a consulting firm, the McChrystal Group. I was sure our members would enjoy learning from him.

McChrystal was receptive when I reached out. He said he wanted the CEOs on the exemplar trip to jog the Washington monuments with him. "It's my favorite thing. We get up first thing in the morning at sunrise, bus in, then break into groups of walkers, joggers, and runners, led by members of my team. At each monument we tell a story about the leader it celebrates—Lincoln, Jefferson, Washington, Martin Luther King Jr., Roosevelt."

That sounded fantastic, and very Tugboat, to me. About thirty members signed up. Because McChrystal could give us only one day, I asked my former UC Berkeley roommate, Rob Shenk, to host us for a day at Mount Vernon where they could learn about George Washington as a practitioner of the Evergreen 7Ps principles. He readily agreed and invited a couple of historians of the first president to join us.

The visit was a success. Afterward, we went back to McChrystal's office and spent the rest of the day learning from him. As we reviewed key concepts in his most recent book, *Team of Teams: New Rules of Engagement for a Complex World*, I couldn't help but notice the 7Ps and Evergreen in general coming through. For team building, he talked about the critical importance of adaptability and extreme information transparency combined with rapid, decentralized decision-making at the lowest level possible. I couldn't help but think of the SRC meetings and financials pasted on the walls, and the scrap metalworker who made a decision that became a business unit.

That evening we had barbecue at McChrystal's house complete with a keg of beer in the garage. One of my fondest memories is of that night, sitting around the keg while the general filled our cups and told us stories.

Two weeks later, I sat on a panel about building companies to last a hundred years or more, joined by the owners of two Evergreen companies, Amy Simmons of Amy's Ice Cream in Austin and Rich Panico of Integrated Project Management in Chicago. Afterward, John Garrett of Community Impact, a newspaper business based in Texas, who has since become a stalwart of Tugboat Institute, approached me wondering why I hadn't responded to his application to join Tugboat. "I just never heard back," he said. A dozen or more attendees who had approached me after the talk said the same.

We poked around with our developers to discover they had goofed. The applications weren't stored in a database as they should have been. What was worse was they hadn't kept activity logs on the site, which is Web 101 stuff. All we had was the most recent records, and that showed six or seven applications in the last two days we'd missed.

I was floored. The article had been out for a month! Had we missed 50 applications? 100? 150? Whatever the number, the debacle felt at the time like the capstone to a tough, up-and-down year, from the struggle to put on the third Tugboat Institute Summit to the loss of potential members that could have gotten us to breakeven or, better, profitability. We would get there, but I still wonder how many applications I missed and how far it set us back. It was as if, after two great years, we were suddenly cursed.

And yet, as frustrating as the website fiasco was, I can see in retrospect that we had crossed a threshold by that point. The article did bring in about twenty-five new members, and similar to IDEO's experience, it became an invaluable calling card to explain ourselves to curious leaders.

At the same time, I realized part of the problems we'd faced were from my bifurcated attention. I was working like mad to grow Tugboat Institute while still doing my job with leading Tugboat Ventures, where I still had responsibilities to the companies I'd invested in and our limited partners. I needed help or we'd face more fiascoes like the ones we'd faced since Chris left. I brought it a new CFO, Dan Benetz, to help put processes in place and codify our operations—the things required to scale an organization.

Growth followed. I was freed up to do my Tugboat Ventures job and spend all my other time spreading the word on Evergreen companies through speeches and interviews. I was also spending a fair bit of time continuing to expand my own understanding of the Evergreen way of doing business and identifying more Evergreen companies—whether or not they were members of Tugboat Institute.

For a year or more, I had seesawed between moments of elation—when I could see this other way of doing business, talk to the people doing it and learn from them, and increase my conviction in Evergreen—and moments of doubt that Evergreen wasn't what I had built up in my mind. It was when we secured over fifty paying members that it became finally, fully clear, that this was not something I had overhyped in my head. It was a not a cute little niche. It was real. There were many more Evergreen companies and Evergreen leaders than I had imagined. I began to see them wherever I looked.

PART THREE

THE
EVERGREEN
ADVANTAGE

10

A Forest of Evergreens

The world I grew up in—of VC and startups—conspires to shield us from the thriving and diverse world of private companies. The structure of business education and the culture that celebrates rapid, personal wealth generation above a business's contributions to its community and society are coconspirators in this. Even before VC moved to get-big-fast, the long-standing view in businesses, private equity, venture capital, and academia was deeply entrenched: going public should be the highest aspiration of every company. It is the goal. And, if not public, then sold at a very high price. Anything in contravention to that goal is neither celebrated nor studied with any zeal.

So, private companies, even large ones, just don't tend to attract as much media or scholarly attention as the public titans. Certainly, it was a blind spot for me. As you can see in my journey to Evergreen companies, there were moments when incredibly smart ideas about how to run a business simply weren't registering with me because they made no sense *if the goal is to go public or be sold*. It's why, for months, I harbored doubts about what I sensed—that there is another way to build businesses that are meaningful and last. It took three summits, two exemplar visits, and dozens upon dozens of conversations with people in this world of well-run private enterprise for me to fully accept that the Evergreen company concept was real. And once I did, I discovered that a surprisingly large number of private companies met our criteria of practicing the Evergreen 7Ps principles, which, let me remind you, are:

- Purpose

- Perseverance

- People First

- Private

- Profit

- Paced Growth

- Pragmatic Innovation

What's more, the longer I talked about this idea, the less I needed to even go looking for Evergreen leaders and companies. They started coming to me.

David Weekley, for example, is the founder and chairman of the celebrated home-building company that bears his name. One day, he called me out of the blue. He had seen a list of the Evergreen 7Ps principles, and they perfectly described the way he and his associates had built David Weekley Homes over the previous forty years. He wanted to know if he could use the 7Ps on his website. I think he was also challenging me to see whether we were serious about this.

I told him that following the 7Ps was requisite for Tugboat Institute companies and I'd be happy to let him use them on his website if he joined. And he did, although he never attended any of our events. Later, Chris, the company president and his son, joined, becoming an active member.

In-N-Out Burger is another private company that chose a growth strategy different from its publicly owned fast-food competitors. Compared to other private companies, In-N-Out is known and celebrated (though maybe not studied) for its legion (some call it a cult) of devoted customers. But I didn't realize how Evergreen it was until I came across an excellent book by journalist Stacy Perman, *In-N-Out Burger: A Behind-the-Counter Look at the Fast-Food Chain That Breaks All the Rules*. It turned out that "breaking all the rules" meant operating according to the Evergreen 7Ps principles.

In-N-Out began as the love story of Harry and Esther Snyder, its founders. They had started In-N-Out in 1948 as a simple hamburger stand in their hometown of Baldwin Park, just east of downtown Los Angeles. Their idea was to serve "fast" the freshest, highest-quality hamburgers, fries, and shakes in a sparkling clean environment with an open kitchen and a happy, well-rewarded, and highly appreciated staff of "associates."

Their watchword was "simple." The philosophy: "Do one thing and do it exceptionally well." The Snyders followed it faithfully, down to the cuts of beef they would purchase (only prime chuck) and the parts of a head of lettuce they would use (only the crispiest inside leaves). They were also committed from the start to remaining family owned and independent.

In-N-Out was hardly alone in seeing the fast-food opportunities. Carl's Jr. started in 1941, Jack in the Box in 1951, McDonald's in 1955—all three in Southern California. Chick-fil-A was born in Georgia in 1946, KFC in 1952 in Kentucky, Burger King in Florida in 1953. But unlike any others, Harry and Esther were not interested in growing fast or taking on franchisees or outside investors. In-N-Out grew slowly under the founders and their successors—their two sons and then their granddaughter, the current CEO. After seventy-five years of paced growth, it had about 360 locations in six states, was worth an estimated $3 billion, and did about $575 million in annual revenue, with same-store sales far above other burger chains. In-N-Out stores are, in fact, eagerly sought by communities across the United States. When it announced that it would open its first restaurant east of the Mississippi, just outside Nashville, the news was heralded by the governor of Tennessee.

The Snyders were Pragmatic Innovators. Years before Ray Kroc, for example, they invented the drive-through, as well as the phone system that allowed customers to place their orders as soon as they pulled into the In-N-Out circular driveway. Unfortunately, Harry Snyder did not bother to patent his inventions and thus did not profit as he might have when other companies copied them.

As I continued to discover more and more Evergreen companies, it occurred to me that the largest private company in the United States might also be an Evergreen company. Cargill is that company, and it does $165 billion in annual revenue. It is an integral component of the global food supply chain. All this information was available to me in B-school, through a friend who had married a member of the family, but I found it uninteresting back then. My friends and I were focused on tech businesses like Excite and @Home, the latest bright shiny objects in Silicon Valley. Both of those, of course, merged, went public, filed for bankruptcy, and disappeared in the space of six years. Cargill is 130 years old.

In my Evergreen search, I eventually met with Annie MacMillan, my classmate's wife, who was part of the family. The company's purpose statement was one of the most powerful I'd ever heard: "Feed the world."

That's it. And it permeates the family and affects everything the company does. The indoctrination of the children began when they were preteens. I clearly remember her telling me that no one in her family was more important than that purpose, to feed the world.

I can't say for sure if Cargill practices all the Evergreen principles because I don't know enough about its internal operations, but I can be confident about other iconic private companies that were joining Tugboat Institute. Radio Flyer joined when Chief Wagon Officer (and CEO) Robert Pasin learned about us through another member.

Robert's grandfather, Antonio Pasin, founded the company in 1917. As a young Italian immigrant in Chicago, he had started out making phonograph cabinets but branched out into other products including a coaster wagon that soon became such a hot seller that he switched to full-scale wagon production.

Under Antonio and then his son, Mario, the company became famous around the world for its iconic red wagons manufactured in Chicago. In 1997, Antonio's grandson and Mario's son Robert became CEO. Recognizing that consumer tastes were changing, Robert saw a need to begin making products out of molded plastic instead of just the traditional steel and wood. He was, however, unable to convince the union in the factory to make the change, and so Radio Flyer began outsourcing its manufacturing of molded plastic wagons while refocusing its internal efforts on product development. It also became very serious about making itself a great place to work and was repeatedly recognized as one by media outlets.

Those were the two Ps—Pragmatic Innovation and People First policies—that I wanted to delve into when we took about fifty members of Tugboat Institute on an exemplar visit to Radio Flyer.

On the first matter, what struck me was something that Radio Flyer did *not* have, a product picker.

In Silicon Valley, there had been a mystique about product pickers—people with the uncanny ability to identify new products that would have mass appeal. Steve Jobs was the quintessential example. PalmPilot and Handspring creator Jeff Hawkins, whom I had worked with at Good Technology, was another. It's a rare thing because it's quite hard to nail what customers will want once, never mind again and again. I experienced this in my time with board games when I was on the Cranium board while at TPG.

Radio Flyer's chief innovation officer, Tom Schlegel, explained the company's product selection process. He showed us a slide with images of products—wagons, tricycles, collapsible stuff, and so on—and a line dividing them right down the middle. He challenged us to explain how those on one side were different from those on the other.

We couldn't do it. Individual products certainly were different, but as groups, the two batches looked the same. So Schlegel explained. He pointed to the batch on the left side of the line. "The ones on this side were all extremely successful, our bestsellers." He then pointed to the other side. "The ones on the right were complete failures."

Radio Flyer had replaced a product picker with a system that reminded me of the innovation process I'd learned about at SAS Institute—digging a lot of little holes. Robert's metaphor was seeds. "We've got to plant a lot of seeds because we don't know which ones are going to take root and grow up to be a successful product." The company would roll out low-cost prototypes of new products to customers, retailers, and distributors with the aim of getting some market feedback before ramping up production and investing in inventory.

Robert confessed that the system was fallible. Sometimes the early market test suggested a winner that subsequently flopped. Other times, apparent duds were shut down, but maybe they would have bucked the market test. They would never know. What Robert did know, he said, was that "whenever we've had such a strong opinion about a product that we decided to disregard early warning signs from the market, we were almost always disappointed. Those failures brought us back to the importance of having a replicable process not dependent on any one human being."

Radio Flyer's chief people officer, Amy Bastuga, explained how the company developed the practices that turned it into a "best place to work." She brought to life for us the dozens of techniques the company uses to foster a team mentality among employees. It reminded me of something that Kleiner Perkins partner Will Hearst (now chairman of the Hearst Corporation) had told me years before, that the competitive advantage that people underestimate is the accumulation of the thousands of little things that a company has learned to do well, things that it's impossible to replicate in a startup that hasn't even had time to establish a system.

It struck me that I was seeing exactly what Will had talked about in Radio Flyer's hundreds of People First practices. They included the tiniest details. How were new employees greeted when they showed up for their first day on the job? What was sitting on their desks? What happened in the first week? How were they evaluated? Robert brought out a couple of very large corkboards covered with documents describing every aspect of the employee experience that Radio Flyer practices. He gave our members copies to use however they saw fit. "Just take off the Radio Flyer logos," he said, "but feel free to plagiarize them as much as you like."

In the time we spent with Robert, I couldn't help noticing the deep connection he felt with his grandfather, Antonio, who had taken all the risks involved in building the company in the 1920s and 1930s. One of the biggest was an exhibit he created for the 1933 "Century of Progress" World's Fair in Chicago. With help from a friend, he constructed a forty-five-foot-high "coaster boy" pulling a giant Radio Flyer wagon. It was so expensive that if it hadn't brought in a significant amount of new business, the company probably would have folded. Fortunately, it was one of the most popular exhibits at the fair, where, among other things, visitors could buy miniature Radio Flyers for twenty-five cents.

Clearly, Antonio Pasin was not only a craftsman but a natural marketer. His grandson is as well. I could see that he regards Radio Flyer as a trust of which he is now steward. It's as if, in addition to his ownership, he has a responsibility to uphold the honor of something that is part of his family's heritage and his own identity. More Ps: Private. Purpose. Perseverance.

I have noticed this same sense of stewardship in other leaders of the many multigeneration Evergreen family businesses (more than half of our members) that have joined Tugboat Institute. They included Val Hollingsworth III of Hollingsworth & Vose (H&V), a Massachusetts manufacturer of "nonwoven materials and engineered paper products" that can trace its roots back to 1728 when a group of colonial Bostonians received permission from the Massachusetts Bay Colony to set up a paper mill so that colonists wouldn't have to import all their paper from England. In 1798, they brought in an apprentice, Mark Hollingsworth, who in time took over the mill while was also raising a large family. He eventually gave the original mill to his oldest son, while he himself took out a mortgage on his home and bought the Revere Copper Works from the family of Paul Revere. He then started another company with two of his younger sons. That company became Hollingsworth & Vose in 1881 when Mark's descendant, Zackery, formed a partnership with a dynamic sales manager named Charles Vose.

Both before and after that transition, Hollingsworth & Vose survived and grew by Pragmatic Innovation, making specialized paper products for industrial customers. Today, most of what the company makes goes into batteries or filters. A few decades ago, it did many, many more industrial products, but it has narrowed its focus.

Val Hollingsworth himself joined H&V in 1976 and became CEO in 1988, a post he held until 2022, when he moved to his current role of chairman. During his tenure, the company grew from two mills in Massachusetts and two more in upstate New York to an international operation with thirteen locations, adding China, India, Germany, England, and Mexico. Its direct customers are the manufacturers of filters, which sell in turn to companies such as Tesla and SpaceX. It's remarkable to think of a company that has persevered long enough to serve both Ben Franklin and Elon Musk.

Most impressive has been H&V's ability to finance all that growth out of retained earnings and bank loans. As Val likes to point out, the company has not sold equity—that is, brought in outside capital investors—in more than a hundred years.

. . .

I sometimes wonder how many people in Silicon Valley know anything about these companies and others like them. I wonder how interested they'd be if we chatted about it at a dinner party. Considering how long it took me to separate myself from the conventional wisdom—going public is the endgame; outside capital is necessary for success; the faster and bigger the better—I figured many would stare at me blankly or wander off looking for what they thought would be a better conversation. They can't see there's another way.

But I had hope some would come around, and I had evidence somewhere, in academia at least. In 2016, amid this great growth in Tugboat Institute and in my view of the thriving world of Evergreen businesses, Spencer Burke, an adjunct professor in family business at the Olin Business School of Washington University in St. Louis, reached out to inquire about our work. Our work dovetailed with his own in his course on "The Competitive Advantage of Family and Employee-Owned Firms." He was also a principal of the St. Louis Trust Company, whose clientele were largely owners of family businesses, many that seemed to be Evergreen companies, which he has introduced to me.

One of them is Stupp Bros. Inc., a 165-year-old Evergreen business that today is a pillar of the St. Louis community. The current CEO is John P. Stupp Jr., the great-great grandson of Johann Stupp, a German immigrant who founded a predecessor company called J. Stupp & Bros., Blacksmiths, in 1856. It later changed its name to South St. Louis Ironworks. All three of Johann's sons worked there when the financial Panic of 1873 hit, triggering what became known as the Long Depression. Johann had borrowed $3,000 from a lender, who called in the loan. When Johann couldn't pay it back, he lost the company.

Perhaps chastened by the experience, Johann's eldest son, George, had begun taking business classes. In 1878, he launched a company he called the George Stupp South St. Louis Ornamental Zinc and Iron Works. When his younger brothers, Peter and Julius, came of age, he brought them in as partners and changed the name to Stupp Bros. They began building bridges as Stupp Bros. Bridge & Iron Company. It has continued to prosper ever since, building infrastructure all over the country. Today Stupp Bros. Inc. has four subsidiaries: Stupp Bridge Company, Ben Hur Construction Co., Stupp Fiber (broadband), and Midwest BankCentre, a community bank.

I met John Stupp Jr. in 2017 in the elegant dining room of the Ritz-Carlton near St. Louis. I was struck that he talked as if the events he detailed from the company's long history had happened the year before, even if they happened more than a century earlier. He expressed them as clear memories and currently relevant. Because his family had been there the whole time, he had the wisdom of the prior generations to draw on, what had worked and what hadn't. Most companies that go through ownership transitions don't have that advantage. Once they're sold and the guard changes, the accumulated wisdom is lost.

One of the experiences that stayed with the family was Johann Stupp's loss of the company due to the loan he couldn't repay during the Long Depression. After restarting the business, his successors vowed that they would never let it happen again and forswore taking on debt. Over the 140 years following the bankruptcy, Stupp Brothers grew to about $250 million in annual revenue without borrowing money or selling equity—especially remarkable given that its business was the construction of bridges and other large structures.

I didn't realize at the time that I was receiving my next big lesson in what it means to be an Evergreen company. Stupp and Wash U's Spencer Burke got me in touch with another family business, Enterprise Mobility, the parent company of Enterprise Rent-A-Car, National Car Rental, and Alamo Rent a Car. We eventually reached former CEO and current Executive Chairman Andrew Taylor, who readily agreed to host us for another Tugboat exemplar visit.

11

Big Evergreens

E nterprise is an extraordinary Evergreen company.

Jack Taylor joined the navy in 1942 and become a fighter pilot in the Pacific, earning two Distinguished Flying Crosses and the Navy Air Medal. After the war, he returned home to St. Louis and landed a job as sales manager at Lindburg Cadillac. After a decade there, he saw an opportunity and persuaded his boss, Arthur Lindburg, to join him in launching Executive Leasing Company (ELS), in 1957. They had seven cars customers could rent when their own cars were being repaired. By 1969, ELS branched out from St. Louis into other states. Taylor couldn't use the "Executive" name in some markets, so he rebranded as Enterprise Leasing Company, using the name of the aircraft carrier—the USS *Enterprise*—he'd served on in the war. It became Enterprise Rent-A-Car in 1989.

Unlike other rental car companies, which focused on the business and leisure markets with service at airports, Jack had identified another untapped market for car rental, which he called the "home-city" market. It was for people who needed cars where they lived and worked. Enterprise put offices in neighborhoods and came to dominate this market.

From the beginning, Jack Taylor built the company on a simple philosophy: Take care of your customers and employees first, and profits will follow. Its customer service became legendary, and Enterprise reinforced the message with its slogan: "We'll Pick You Up." His son Andrew followed the same philosophy when he took over as president in the early 1980s. The company's revenue was $78 million at the time. When he moved up from president to CEO in 1991, it approached $1 billion. By the time of our visit in 2018, Enterprise Holdings was doing $24 billion in annual sales, with a global fleet of 2 million vehicles.

I had come to appreciate how many of the Evergreen companies I visited or learned about were able to grow without IPOs or outside capital, but this was the next level, and it impressed me immensely. This is a capital-intensive business, and Enterprise grew from $78 million to $24 billion while staying private and never raising outside capital. The math only works if you're incredibly skillful at managing inventory—that is, buying, selling, and maintaining cars and trucks in a way that allows you to maximize the efficient use of your capital.

The ninety-two Tugboat Institute members and I who went to St. Louis for two days of meetings and tours wanted to know how they did it.

We began, as we usually do, with a "fireside chat" with Andy Taylor. He was executive chairman at that point. He talked about the tremendous growth that began shortly after he became president in 1980. "In fact, in the early '80s, we went too fast," he said. "We didn't have enough talented leaders. That proved to be a great lesson about not getting ahead of your leadership. We had to double back over the next couple of years and restart." This was Paced Growth.

His problem, if you can call it that, was the abundance of opportunities he and his team identified in the home-city market. When I asked him why he kept opening offices after reaching a size that would have given him a comfortable lifestyle, he said he was having too much fun to stop. "I just always really liked the business. Like my father, I work with fun people for the most part. We saw opportunities, particularly in the car rental space. Later we'd add a car leasing service. It seemed natural. It was fun. It was exciting. I was never a big golfer. Business is sort of my hobby. People say, 'You must love cars. Do you collect them?' I say, 'I collect cars that produce revenue.'"

Andy explained that Enterprise got to its current size only because of the foundation laid by his father, Jack, who had based it on his experience in the navy. There he learned that the four key factors determining success were service, mission, teamwork, and fun. These were adapted for the business by Jack as four tenets for success:

First, make sure customers have a good experience.

Second, bring in the best people you can find, give them tools, develop them, and make them your future leaders.

Third, provide continual growth to create opportunities that will keep everyone interested and engaged.

Fourth, maintain a reasonable bottom line while staying private.

For the first tenet, Andy invented a tool called the Enterprise Service Quality Index (ESQI). In the 1980s, when the company was growing fast, Jack and Andy began hearing from friends about people who hadn't had a good experience with Enterprise. The Taylors were disappointed and baffled. Why was this happening?

Andy's initial response was to send customers an eighteen-question survey, "which is exactly the wrong way to do it," he told us. "Nobody sent the eighteen questions back." So they adjusted and instead sent just three questions:

- How satisfied are you with your experience on a scale of one (completely unsatisfied) to five (completely satisfied)?

- The next time you rent a car, would you choose Enterprise?

- Is there anything else you want to tell us?

Later, they'd ask these questions by phone. Beginning in 1989, Andy required every office to administer the ESQI and calculate a score based on the percentage of customers feeling "completely satisfied"—that is, giving a five in response to that first, crucial question. He then shared the results with the entire workforce, figuring that the natural competitiveness of Enterprise's people would lead them to improve their scores.

But it didn't. After four years, Andy talked to his father about his frustration that the scores weren't improving. "Give them the stick," Jack said. He meant create negative consequences for lower scores.

So, Andy made a new policy: to be eligible for promotion or rewards and recognition, the ESQI score of a branch had to be equal to or higher than the corporate average. Scores were based solely on "completely satisfied" answers, because completely satisfied customers turned out to be three times more likely than satisfied customers to come back and rent again.

It worked. The company's percentage of completely satisfied customers rose from the mid-sixties to the mid-eighties. Those employees in branches who didn't meet or exceed the average were denied promotions and bonuses for as long as their scores remained below the corporate average. They called it "ESQI jail."

This system might sound familiar to some readers. Fred Reich-held of Bain & Company adopted it from Enterprise and featured it in his book *The Ultimate Question*. He called it the net pro-moter score. One of the most popular tools in business over the past forty years was lifted from an Evergreen company.

Enterprise doesn't hire from competitors. "You may be able to grow a little faster when you buy leadership from other companies—like Hertz or Avis, in our case—but we discovered very quickly that their goals and businesses are different from ours," Andy said. "When we brought people in from those companies, we couldn't deprogram them and make them interested in our four tenets. So, we gave that up real fast."

Instead, Enterprise recruits heavily from recent college gradu-ates, especially those with a strong extracurricular record. What attracts the graduates is Enterprise's reputation for providing world-class training and choosing its future leaders from within. In effect, they are being hired to start a career, not do a job. It's a form of the long-lost employment "contract" based on mutual loyalty and commitment between employer and employee. That contract scarcely exists anymore elsewhere in the US economy—and certainly not in Silicon Valley—but it is alive and well in Ever-green companies like Enterprise.

In the mid-aughts, Enterprise branched out from the home-city market and acquired National and Alamo rental car companies, airport-based outfits that were strong in the more traditional busi-ness and leisure rental market.

My experience with acquisitions was that the buyer would ba-sically make over what it bought: install its own executive team, switch information systems and reporting procedures, impose its way of doing business, and force everyone to adapt.

Enterprise didn't do that. A handful of senior people from En-terprise moved over to National and Alamo, and they didn't sack the existing management or try to change the culture. Instead, they observed, eventually concluding that both companies were quite well run. They appreciated that the target customers of National (businesspeople in a hurry) and Alamo (cost-conscious travelers) were fundamentally different from Enterprise customers. Both companies, they realized, had been built and were organized to accommodate their respective clienteles, and the main role Enterprise could play would be to help them do what they already did, but better.

This contrasted so sharply with the usual playbook, but when you match it to Enterprise's four tenets, it makes sense. If you buy a company and your first tenet is to make sure your customers have a good experience, you naturally must start by finding out who your new customers are and then providing them with what *they* want, not whatever service or product you're accustomed to delivering. And in the case of the public company, the demands of a public market will require you to create synergies, which means cost cutting in the form of consolidation, integration, increased efficiencies, and layoffs.

So much of the conventional wisdom I had learned in Silicon Valley that was being overthrown seemed counterintuitive at first, but then you realize it's not at all when the core values and behaviors at Evergreen companies, honed over decades or centuries, are as ingrained in them as get-big-fast or growth-at-all-costs are ingrained in VCs over the past twenty-eight years. Evergreen eaders are as surprised by the Valley way of doing business as I sometimes found myself early on by the Evergreen way.

The acquisition of National and Alamo made Enterprise the largest car rental company in the world, proof positive of something that, in the early days of my search, many people had told me I would never find. *There are no big Evergreen companies, Dave*, doubters would tell me. *It's a small-company phenome-*

non. You simply cannot, in today's world, build a big company without raising venture capital or private equity.

Wrong. Enterprise was a $24 billion Evergreen colossus. It's four tenets can be mapped to Evergreen 7Ps. Let's look again.

> First, make sure customers have a good experience: Pragmatic Innovation.

> Second, bring in the best people you can find, give them tools, develop them, and make them your future leaders: People First.

> Third, provide continual growth to create opportunities that will keep everyone interested and engaged: Paced Growth.

> Fourth, maintain a reasonable bottom line while staying private: Profit and Private.

I couldn't help but wonder how Andy had done it. What personal qualities had allowed him to grow his company from $78 million to $24 billion in annual sales in thirty-eight years? "Focus," he said.

"Focus?"

"Yes, I'm not the smartest person the room, but I have the ability to focus at a level that most people can't," he said. "And I can focus for very long periods of time."

I thought back to some of the smart people I'd worked with in Silicon Valley. For them, focus was not a quality that came to mind. They were certainly clever and creative. They were always trying out new things, adding complexity to whatever they were trying to do. But in the search for ideas, it's easy to get distracted and pulled in new directions—to lose focus. A core startup process in the Valley is to "pivot," which is another way to say, "change your focus, fast."

"We do a lot of little experiments, too," Andy said, echoing the digging of little holes or planting of many seeds. "We always want to improve, but we also understand exactly what business we are in. I knew it from when I started here in St. Louis: if I could take what we did well to other markets, we would do well there, too, and I never tired of that focus. I never tired of buying cars. I never tired of renting cars. I never tired of customer service. I don't get bored. Most CEOs don't have the attention span to dedicate four decades of their life to doing the same thing over and over and doing it really, really well."

As we spoke, I could feel his focus on me. His eyes were steely. It was as if his energy was flying out at me, and I could feel it. *Wow, if I were on his team . . .* , I thought. I really got it. And I thought it was really cool.

. . .

Enterprise was not the only giant Evergreen company, either. Before joining the St. Louis Trust Company in 2007, Spencer Burke had spent eight years as a general partner in investment banking at Edward Jones, a financial advisory company with $13.5 billion annual revenue and $2 trillion of assets under management, also based in St. Louis.

I was skeptical that a financial services company could be an Evergreen one. I knew of only one exception, Capital Group, with $2.6 trillion of assets under management, featured in the book *Capital: The Story of Long-Term Investment Excellence*, by Charles D. Ellis.

When Burke told me Edward Jones was like Capital Group, I took notice. And in it I had found another big Evergreen. Edward Jones has been around almost a hundred years. It's had five

CEOs. It's owned by its partners, both current and retired, without an ESOP.

Jim Weddle was managing partner (that's what they call the CEO). With Burke, I met him at their headquarters, and he confirmed the Evergreen 7Ps principles hewed to his firm's practices.

I also spoke with Bob Ciapciak, a partner who functioned as Weddle's chief of staff. He asked if I was familiar with Peter Drucker of the Claremont Graduate School, described by *Businessweek* as "the man who invented management." Of course, I said.

"Well, Peter Drucker and the Edward Jones leadership team were very close," Ciapciak said. "Every quarter we visited him in Claremont and talked about some of the things we were dealing with. He had such a brilliant mind and the ability to see things so clearly. He told us we had done the best job of any company in the world in adopting his leadership principles throughout the organization, which wasn't an accident." Ciapciak went to a bookshelf and brought back a copy of Drucker's *The Effective Executive*, which he gave me. "Every single person in this organization has this book, and we expect them all to read it and understand it."

I had read it about fifteen years earlier. That weekend I read it again. I later sent a copy to every member of Tugboat Institute.

Based on what I saw during my visit, I wasn't surprised to find out that Edward Jones, like other Evergreens, had appeared year after year on the Great Place to Work list in *Fortune*. But there was something new at this company I hadn't seen at other Evergreens, a bold choice by the founder's son to change its ownership structure.

Edward D. Jones Sr. started the firm in 1922 in a one-room office in downtown St. Louis. His son Ted joined in 1948 as its eighteenth broker, initially based in the suburb of Clayton. In 1957, the firm opened its first branch office in Mexico, Missouri, about two hours northwest of St. Louis.

Forty-six years later, in 1968, Ted Jones took over as managing partner. He expanded aggressively outside of St. Louis, setting up small offices throughout the rural Midwest, all of which could operate with just a single financial adviser and their assistant. Ted also believed that Edward Jones should be owned by its associates, rather than his family—contrary to his father's plan to extend partnership to Ted's two sisters, who did not work in the firm. Giving partners a personal stake in the company's success would, he thought, encourage them to put all their attention into providing great service to customers.

This was astonishing. Ted could easily have taken the company public, given its aggressive growth. If he did that, he could have cashed out his stake worth hundreds of millions of dollars. Instead, he stayed private and meted out ownership to his current and new partners, convinced that it was best for the long-term future of the firm and its clients.

It was a gift that the partners still talk about with obvious gratitude. I attended an annual meeting where I heard partners saying things like, "We wouldn't be here today without the generosity of Ted Jones." His selfless act no doubt played a role in fostering the strong spirit of volunteerism at the company. You can see it, for example, in the mentoring program that Edward Jones's people donate their time to, which has increased the firm's ability to bring in more associates from diverse backgrounds.

Bob Ciapciak asked if I could come back for their annual partners meeting, where I would interview a speaker for the event. They had in mind Danny Wegman, chairman of Wegmans, the East Coast supermarket chain. I suggested we consider Danny's daughter Colleen, who'd been CEO for eighteen months. She agreed to the interview.

Wegmans Food Markets was founded in 1916 in Rochester, New York, by brothers John and Walter Wegman. Today it has 53,000 employees, 110 stores in locations from Massachusetts to Virginia, and $12 billion in annual revenues, making it the thirty-eighth largest private company in the country, as well as another perennial occupant of the Great Place to Work list. Another big Evergreen.

As eager as I was to do the interview with Colleen, I didn't feel prepared. I had never set foot in a Wegmans because I didn't live or spend much time in its regions. I was aware how highly regarded it was by its industry peers and by friends of mine who had shopped there. "Until you walk into a Wegmans, Dave, you can't get it," one of them told me. "It's an experience. You're not just shopping. You're being educated. They do things like teaching you how to cook. It's not just a grocery store. It's a place where they help people learn how to prepare the healthiest and best-tasting meals for their families."

One of Colleen Wegman's directors hooked me up, at my request, with every bit of background they had on the company: HR policies, statement of values, history of the company, training materials, industry reports. As I plowed through it, my esteem for the company grew. It was easy to understand why the company had always been on the Great Place to Work list, but I realized that its greatness wasn't just a function of its People First practices. It could also be seen in the quality of its products, its customer service, and the in-store experience—all areas in which Wegmans was constantly, pragmatically innovating.

I finally met Colleen in person shortly before the partners meeting where I'd be interviewing her. As Colleen gave her half-hour remarks about Wegmans, I was reminded of In-N-Out Burger, in that both companies had been built around a core set of values having to do with product, customers, and employees, rather than the priorities of shareholders.

My first question in our interview went right at one of the Evergreen 7Ps—Paced Growth. "Colleen, there are cities all over this country that would do whatever you asked if you'd open a store in their area. But you guys just add *two* stores per year, and for the first eighty years of your existence you operated only in the state of New York. Why haven't you taken advantage of the many other opportunities you've had to scale up? What is holding you back? Is it a financial issue?"

"No, no, no, it's not that at all," she said. "It's about our people. It's about the way, as a family, we want to open stores in communities. We found that when we opened two stores a year, we could do it well. We bring in people from existing stores as the core of the startup team. We complement them with local folks, whom we train. My family is there, too. There's a whole launch process, including a merchandising plan that's customized to that specific area. It takes time and a lot of effort to get it right. One year, we tried opening *three* stores, and it just didn't work for us. So, we went back to doing two a year."

"But you're so much bigger now. Adding two stores per year when you have thirty is one thing. Adding two when you're up to almost a hundred stores is another matter."

"Dave, that pace—two new stores per year—is just the way we've had success with and the way we want to build the company we have and love."

I got the message. Even now, fully immersed in Evergreen companies and Evergreen culture, I sometimes found myself reflecting back to old ways of thinking. My brain was just automatically doing the calculations—*you're three times as big now, so you can open three times more stores per year.* But a lack of capital was not holding back Wegmans' growth nor was a dearth of attractive locations. Wegmans could grow faster but *it chooses not to.* It chose Paced Growth. It accounts for the negative effect on the Wegmans' culture and customer experience a more aggressive expansion may have. I imagine some of my old Valley colleagues will view this as weakness or somehow cowardly and feeble for a company not to chase growth at all costs. So your stores are a little worse at what they do for a while; so your employees don't have a consistently good experience at all locations. You'll more than make up for it in the greatly increased value of the company.

Now, after all this time with these companies, that point of view was starting to look like the worse one to me. I was coming to admire Paced Growth as a virtuous kind of discipline. Wegmans stuck to the plan. It wasn't motivated by money alone. It could have made more money by adding more stores, but at some point, for a culture like Wegmans, that's just greed, and it's dangerous. Evergreen companies want to be around forever. Paced Growth from one's own Profit is a better path to longevity, and it's a luxury it wouldn't have if Wegmans were public or a private equity–backed outfit.

I was also impressed by the attention Wegmans paid to local suppliers and the source of everything it carries in each store, as well as the highly personalized experience it wants a customer to have while shopping. When you walk up to the cheese section, for example, you're greeted by somebody who is an expert in all the cheeses in the cabinet, including local ones that are available only in that store. You can get as many samples as you like. It's the sort of service you would expect in a dedicated cheese shop or a boutique market like Zingerman's Deli, but I'd never heard about it happening at the chain supermarket scale.

It all goes back to the company's Purpose: "Helping you live a healthier, better life through food." Colleen told us, for example, that one year the company had taught ten thousand employees to do "pan-searing"—cooking on high heat with salt, pepper, and oil—which they could then teach to customers. But the lessons were not only for the sake of the customers. "We believe we have to have opportunities for our people to learn and grow, and since we're in the food business, it's important that we all connect around food. This connects them to our mission. Every year we pick something to learn about food. We're teaching employees to be healthy." The approach resonates. Employees love working at Wegmans, and the demand for gaining access to jobs there is intense.

And, amazingly, it's happening in the grocery business, an industry under intense competition and economic duress from disruptors outside the business—Amazon, Walmart, Costco, Hello Fresh, Uber Eats, and so many more. Wegmans persists, though, with a different definition of what a grocery store should be. It's a four-generation-old, privately owned business, run by the great-granddaughter of a cofounder. An Evergreen company to the core.

12

Evergreens' Nine Rules
of Innovation

For twelve years, I had been building Tugboat Institute and at the same time unlearning all the knowledge and conventional wisdom I'd absorbed for decades in Silicon Valley.

It took a long time for me to overcome the dogma—*fast growth and scale are fundamental to success; outside capital fuels that growth; going public is the highest calling of a company*—and learn that there is another way, a better way to build successful, enduring businesses. It was not a niche. It was not a few fluky and small companies that were operating with the Evergreen 7Ps principles. Massive companies were doing it, too. Ones not *valued* at a billion dollars—the venture capital unicorns—but ones that were *earning* billions in revenues and growing, from happy customers. And over the long term—a length I hadn't even considered would matter, decades or centuries—they were outperforming many of the darling startups I and my venture capital peers spent years funding and advising.

Enterprise, Edward Jones, and Wegmans were cappers for me—the final proof that had shown me that the Evergreen principles were for any company of any size in any industry. In almost all markets, moreover, Evergreen companies could become the leading players by harnessing the power of compounding Paced Growth. Granted, it may not happen fast. As with Enterprise, it might take decades or even generations to become the leader. But precisely because the growth occurs over time, the companies don't outstrip their culture, management capability, or cash resources as they become large, impactful businesses.

I'm now convinced that Evergreen companies constitute not simply a heretofore unheralded and largely unnoticed type of business but a significant economic force that will be shaping our world far into the future. And they are positioned to make their greatest contribution through innovation.

Through my time building and funding companies, and learning from Evergreen leaders and companies, I've distilled their opportunity and power to innovate into nine innovation lessons that ensure they continue to learn and adapt, remain relevant for decades, if not centuries. Here they are.

Innovation lesson 1: Get risks up front and out early. Identify the four types of risks of an innovation venture—market, tech, team, and financing. Above all, attack market risks. Have little tolerance for them. After a clear-eyed risk assessment, use your and your team's early time and limited resources to remove the white-hot risks as early in the process as possible. If you can't, then don't proceed further. If you can, continue to invest. I learned this from the old guard at Kleiner Perkins. Long before the dot-com era and get-big-fast, Kleiner's Laws aligned in some ways with Evergreen principles. Evergreen companies reintroduced me to this idea. They're very good at this out of necessity. It's their risk, not outside capital's, so they *must* remove the major risks.

Innovation lesson 2: Drive creativity through constraint. My favorite example is the success of the Wright brothers in winning the race to build the first piloted, powered, heavier-than-air flying machine. Owners of a small bicycle shop in Dayton, Ohio, they had little money and far fewer resources generally than any of the others attempting the same feat. Their main competitor, Samuel Langley, was the third secretary of the Smithsonian Institution and had grants of $70,000 (or about $2.5 million in 2023 dollars) from both the Smithsonian and the War Department, as well as any help he wanted from government and academia.

While Langley focused on building a large "aerodrome" with a powerful engine that he thought would push it through the air, the Wright brothers were experimenting with gliders that they built themselves and tested on the sand dunes of North Carolina. In the process, they discovered that the charts being widely used to calculate lift were wrong. To get the accurate numbers, they built wind tunnels and put together their own lift charts. The result: the flight of the first piloted airplane in December 1903.

Innovation lesson 3: Try lots of low-cost experiments. I heard this lesson over and over from Evergreen companies and their leaders, whether it was Jim Goodnight of SAS Institute talking about "digging lots of little holes" or Robert Pasin of Radio Flyer "planting many seeds." Jim Collins and Morten Hansen in the book *Great by Choice* used their own metaphor: "Fire bullets, then cannonballs."

Innovation lesson 4: Take learning journeys. Leaders looking for another way to long-term success take the time to explore outside the business for new ideas, for informed criticism, for identifying blind spots, and for learning from people and companies they admire. It's an opportunity available to leaders of Evergreen companies precisely because they don't have the strict time constraints their counterparts in venture- or private equity–backed businesses face. From my experience at Good Technology, I can attest that entrepreneurs in get-big-fast startups have zero time to take year-long, open-ended learning journeys outside the business, no matter how helpful they may seem.

Innovation lesson 5: Look to suppliers for ideas. My colleague Gary Kunkle has observed that Evergreen companies don't just look to their customers for new ideas. They look to suppliers, too. They, after all, have their own R&D, technology insights, internal expertise, and other resources. Together, you and they will be able to identify, design, and produce innovative, high-margin products and services for customers and do more than could be done in isolation. From the suppliers' standpoint, moreover, there is no better long-term partner than an Evergreen company since it can be counted on to be around for the long haul.

Innovation lesson 6: Protect new ideas. This lesson came from the cofounder and former CEO of Pixar, Ed Catmull: protect your new, rough ideas from the financial metrics and requirements of the established business, whose members often have a short memory about what it took for the original business to get to its current state. "[T]hink of how a movie starts out," Catmull wrote in *Creativity Inc.* "It's a baby. . . . [W]e all start out ugly. Every one of Pixar's stories starts out that way. A new thing is hard to define; it's not attractive, and it requires protection. . . . Every new idea in any field needs protection. Pixar is set up to protect our director's ugly baby."

Recent Tugboat member Paul Kambach Jr., of Kambach Feeds Inc., has created *four* new companies under his family business by honoring this lesson.

Innovation lesson 7: Take advantage of your longer investment time horizon. Amazon, though a public company, has repeatedly shown how it can work. Says Bezos, "What we're really focused on is thinking long term, putting the customer at the center of our universe and inventing. Those are the three big ideas to think long term because a lot of invention doesn't work. . . . That's how we do it and, by the way, we have a lot of fun doing it."

Hollingsworth & Vose had this experience with one of its technologies that required a decade of patience to realize its full potential. Now, that tech is in nearly every start/stop battery that's sold.

Innovation lesson 8: Pursue market-creating innovations. My good fortune to be able to spend time with leading innovation scholar Clayton Christensen, prior to his untimely passing in 2020, helped me see this.

Christensen posited three types of innovation in business:

- Performance-enhancing, for example, adding a touch pad to a laptop

- Efficiency-improving, for example, a new just-in-time manufacturing system

- Market-creating, for example, the invention of personal computers

It's the third one that leads to the creation of new industries and thousands, or even millions, of new jobs. Such innovations are disruptive because they inevitably force major changes to behavior, both in the company and with its customers. Evergreens have a unique advantage today because these innovations can happen *only* over time and in stages. The first stage, core development, can take years and involves a small team removing technological risks and testing business models. That leads to establishing the product in a small, foothold market, where it offers a unique and valuable benefit to customers in that market, though the technology hasn't matured enough to compete in large, mainstream markets. Eventually—in seven to twelve years—the product's performance and the company's capabilities mature enough to compete in large, mainstream markets. Thereafter, it's a matter of maintaining success.

Given this sequence of stages, Christensen emphasized the importance of generating profit early on so that you can finance the first seven to twelve years of product and foothold market development without depending on outside funding. "You need impatience for profits; patience for growth," he said. That, of course, is exactly the opposite of what venture capitalists and private equity investors want. Their mantra is grow now, profit later. In particular, VCs, including myself in past years, won't tolerate the second stage, in which the startup targets a small foothold market. A company seeking capital to go after a $50 million foothold as its initial target market would be laughed off Sandhill Road. Counterintuitively, the patience to get all the pieces right in a small market, and to grow from one's own profitability, can lead to growth rates that *increase* as the company moves into larger markets.

Christensen noted this paradox to me. Though traditional investors *love* to talk about how great disruptive innovation is, they fund remarkably few such ventures for these reasons. The current structure of venture capital, largely driven from Silicon

Valley, prohibits what the godfather of innovation says is necessary. Since the dot-com boom, the get-big-fast and growth-at-all-costs playbooks demand entrepreneurs pursue large markets from the start.

It's built into the system. In the venture capital industry, the data shows that one or two grand-slam investments drive all of the returns of any large, ten-year fund. To have a shot at such winners in the time window of their funds, venture capitalists invest in a portfolio of companies, each one going after a huge market that will support a rapidly growing company with a huge exit valuation potential, all in the hope that one or two become the grand-slam winners for that fund.

Evergreen companies do not have the same incentives or face the same pressures, and so they can have longer investment time horizons when it comes to innovation, and they can allow however long it may take for a technology, a team, and a market to develop. They can keep going for years, if necessary, until they get it right.

Innovation lesson 9: *Kaizen.* Organize for continuous improvement. A team aligned on purpose, values, and long-term goals, with everyone contributing their best, is the most powerful competitive advantage you can have. You achieve the alignment by training people to understand financials and business principles, providing them with transparent scorecards, and making sure they all have a stake in the outcome. If you can figure out how to leverage the insights, ideas, and energy of employees throughout the organization, hourly workers as well as supervisors and managers, and invite everyone to help eliminate waste and find ways to improve product and service quality, reduce errors, improve cash flow, and invest more wisely, you can't lose. I've found that this lesson, specifically, is universally inherent in Evergreen companies. It's part of their DNA.

. . .

The Evergreen approach that relies on these nine lessons fosters risk mitigation early on, capital efficiency, continuous improvement, unexpected creativity, and new long-term growth vectors.

This Evergreen innovation playbook would not be at all surprising to the entrepreneurs and venture capitalists who practiced in 1960s, 1970s, 1980s, and early 1990s. Investing a total of about $25 billion in venture capital, they helped to create a whole generation of companies that have shaped the world we live in: Fairchild, FedEx, Cisco Systems, Intel, Apple, Microsoft, Amazon, Google (now Alphabet), Electronic Arts, Southwest Airlines, Sun Microsystems, Starbucks, Tandem Computers, Genentech, and Adobe. Those fifteen companies today generate more than $3 trillion in annual revenue. In contrast, since the dot-com bust in March 2000, one company, Uber Technologies, has raised the same amount of venture capital, $25.2 billion, as all those other companies prior to 2000. Yet it reached only $8 billion in annual revenue with $300 million in losses in 2022.

Four venture capital Hall of Famers—Apple, Microsoft, Amazon, and Alphabet (Google) that are each valued at more than $2 trillion today—collectively raised just $40 million in venture capital between them prior to the IPOs. That gives an inkling of how far out of line with historic success the capital being invested today is.

As great as all those early venture-backed companies are, they have all had initial public offerings and are now owned by shortsighted public shareholders. As such, they are not rewarded for embracing the longer time horizons that Evergreen companies enjoy. With perhaps the exception of an Amazon remaining heavily influenced by Bezos, we are unlikely to see those, or any, public companies produce in the future the disruptive, market-creating innovations that Christensen described in his books. I, for one, see the other way, the Evergreen way, as a natural one for capitalizing on Christensen's wisdom.

13

It's about Time

One of the real benefits of creating Tugboat Institute has been the opportunity to be part of a remarkable community of individuals, which is not surprising given that they all follow the Evergreen 7Ps principles. These are not people who need external validation that they are doing the right thing; they know they're doing the right thing. But we are all humans seeking connection and opportunities to learn, so it's wonderful for them to be surrounded by peers that have a similar set of values and willingness to share openly. I like to say that there's not a single Tugboat Institute member I would not enjoy spending personal time with. If you think about communities you are part of, you realize how rare this is.

As we serve these Evergreen CEOs, presidents, executive chairpersons, and their teams, and lead an Evergreen company movement, we are building Tugboat Institute to be an Evergreen company, too. We are driven by Purpose. We put People First. We use Pragmatic Innovation. We Persevere through difficult times. We will stay Private. Paced Growth is our way. The one P I didn't mention above is Profit. Truthfully, Tugboat Institute didn't qualify as an

Evergreen company until recently. It took us six years to reach profitability and nine years to hit the revenue minimum for membership. But we got there.

And on the tenth anniversary of Tugboat Institute, in 2023, we could look back on a decade of progress as well as some significant challenges. Our greatest test came in early 2020 with the onset of the Covid-19 pandemic. Prior to the first lockdowns, we initiated a weekly Pulse Survey allowing members to share what was happening to their top line and what they were doing to save cash, take care of employees, and get back on offense. Each week, we offered the best information we could find to help them, including webinars where members could share their experiences and talk about how they were adapting, and Evergreen-aligned thought leaders, such as former Starbucks president Howard Behar, could share their wisdom.

Despite restrictions, we managed to maintain our regular schedule of Tugboat Institute Summits and Fall Exemplar Visits—adapted for virtual participation. In the fall of 2020, we held one-day sessions at four different member companies from Austin, Texas; St. Louis, Missouri; Huntsville, Alabama; and Boise, Idaho, with limited in-person attendance while streaming to the rest of the membership. In October 2021, we were welcomed back to St. Louis for our Fall Exemplar Visit at Edward Jones hosted by its managing partner, Penny Pennington.

If you've read this far, you shouldn't be surprised to learn that our members' companies weathered the crisis unusually well, even in hard-hit sectors like events and restaurants. Evergreen companies are built to endure these kinds of shocks. Thanks to the Evergreen 7Ps principles, especially People First and Perseverance, and the companies' general aversion to debt, as well as the alignment and short communication channel between ownership and leadership, they are inherently flexible, adaptable, and resilient and thus can make and act on decisions rapidly—an essential quality in any uncertain, fast-changing environment.

Meanwhile, our membership continued to grow about 15 percent annually, and we'd reached close to 275 by the end of 2024. We were adding new experiences and services, usually in response to member requests. During a break in the program at the 2018 Summit, for example, Bobby Jenkins, owner of ABC Home & Commercial Services in Austin, Texas, called out, "When can I bring my wife and my key executives to this event?"

"Well, we set this up as a peer experience," I said and did a quick poll by show of hands of how many other members would like to have spouses and key executives sharing the current experience with them. There were almost no hands.

Afterward, I asked several members informally about Bobby's idea. There was no doubt that members wanted—and would pay for—an additional annual conference for the key executives and family members, but one that was separate from the original summit. In February 2020, we held our first Tugboat Institute Gathering of Teams in Dallas and have been doing it every year since.

As the movement grew, my own understanding of Evergreen companies grew with it. One of our new members, for example, was CEO Dave Petersen of O.C. Tanner, a ninety-six-year-old company in Salt Lake City whose founder, Obert Tanner, had pioneered the business of employee rewards and recognition. Originally a maker of class rings, pins, and ribbons for high school and college graduates, Tanner turned his attention to the corporate world in the 1940s, making the same sort of jewelry for businesses that wanted to recognize employees. The company was thus strictly a jewelry manufacturer for most of its existence.

But the internet created new opportunities, and the company transformed itself over two decades from 100 percent manufacturing to 95 percent services, offering software solutions for employee recognition and rewards, in addition to its original jewelry and other physical gifts. I asked Petersen how the company had pulled off such a drastic transformation. He said it just started with trying to solve a customer's problem. The customer wanted a better way to stay on top of work anniversaries. If companies could send O.C. Tanner digital files of employees coming up for a major milestone or anniversary, the company could help. There was no sudden revelation or aha moment. It was nothing like the venture capital model where a company would hire fifty engineers and rush out a new product with great fanfare. O.C. Tanner was simply responding to customers who needed help with recognizing employees by offering them, for example, an online catalog of possible rewards.

I was struck by the modesty of his response and, when I visited the company, was equally surprised by the physical layout of the headquarters. Typically, in such hybrid companies, manufacturing teams and the software engineers would hold down their own spaces, often far away from each other, maybe even in separate buildings. But here the two groups were integrated. There was no front of the office or back of the office. Some people were working at their computers, separated by a glass wall from the people manning CNC machines precision-cutting products. It all reflected Obert Tanner's insistence that there be no second-class citizens in the company. I felt a strange sense of familiarity in the space; it brought me back to the Hewlett-Packard factories I worked in from my high school days.

Obert Tanner had brought the same clarity of vision to his plans for the company after his death. He arranged for his 65 percent of the shares—the other 35 percent were owned by his nephew and the nephew's family—to be put into a one-hundred-year trust, under which the company could not be sold, merged, or taken public. The trust would initially have his daughter as sole trustee, then three trustees chosen by the board of directors. Those trustees had to have served on the board for an extended period so that the other directors knew them well enough to be sure they would make decisions aligned with the company's values. Tanner's primary motive for developing the trust, he said, was to protect employees and their jobs from outside owners, who would have brought in their own ideas and priorities that might not align with his.

I had never seen such a carefully thought-out plan to protect a company. It was clever Evergreen thinking. Obert Tanner knew his daughter's character from raising her so wanted her to have all the voting shares while she was able to run the business as sole trustee. The idea of a voting trust isn't unique, but making sure that anyone who serves on that critical board has been vetted over years through their service is unique and smart. Tanner significantly reduced the risk of the voting trust being co-opted by people with unaligned ideas for the future of the company.

Another new member of Tugboat Institute was CEO Lisa Ingram of fast-food hamburger chain White Castle. Before meeting her, I had no idea that White Castle was the first fast-food hamburger chain in the world. It had been founded by Lisa's great grandfather Billy Ingram and his partner, Walter Anderson, in 1921—thirty-four years before McDonald's and twenty-seven years before In-N-Out Burger.

As a West Coaster my whole life, I had never been to any of White Castle's more than 350 locations in the Midwest and New York metropolitan area. I was amazed to learn how the company invented the hamburger bun and the "slider"—two-inch square burgers that initially sold for five cents each and were so easy to eat they "slid" down the throats of customers. Unlike other burgers, each White Castle slider had five holes in it (to cook faster and more evenly) and was steamed on a bed of onions rather than grilled. In 2014, *Time* magazine called White Castle's Original Slider the most influential burger of all time.

Like In-N-Out, the company had always prided itself on the quality of its food and the treatment of its employees. It was decades ahead of its time in offering health insurance for team members, for example, but it shunned any change in its menu. For forty-one years, its restaurants served the same five products—burgers, fries, apple pie, Coca-Cola, and coffee. Its first menu change came in 1962 when it began offering the option of adding a slice of cheese to the slider. That's Paced Growth. And focus.

Yet the White Castle burgers were undeniably popular—so popular, in fact, that customers were buying them in bulk, a practice that mystified Lisa's father, Bill Ingram III, who had taken over in 1979. When he did his annual tour of the shops in the early 1980s, he noticed customers buying twenty sliders at a time—four to eat right there and sixteen to take with them. He asked the customers what they planned to do with all those extra sliders. They said they'd freeze them and heat them up in a microwave later, when a craving hit.

Bill saw a new market—and a potentially huge one—selling sliders retail at grocery stores and in its own shops. To serve the market, the company developed new packaging for multiple sliders under the rubric "Crave." There was a ten-slider Crave Sack, a twenty-slider Crave Clutch (in a box), a thirty-slider Crave Case, and a one-hundred-slider Crave Crate.

It was Lisa Ingram, however, who opened wide the Pragmatic Innovation floodgates when she became president and CEO in 2015. While continuing to serve White Castle's signature beef sliders and fries, the company began offering several new products ranging from crab cake sliders to chicken and shrimp "Nibblers," and Impossible (imitation beef) sliders for vegetarians. It also introduced a robot called Flippy 2 that could handle the deep-fry baskets, and "Julia," an AI for drive-through orders.

The latter it developed in partnership with Mastercard, one of many such arrangements, some of which were forged with White Castle loyalists. Telfar Clemens, for example, is a fashion designer and founder of the label Telfar, not to mention a lifelong craver from Queens. He contacted the company on its toll-free 800-line and introduced himself to Lisa, who saw an opportunity for a partnership by having Telfar design the uniforms employees would wear in 2021 while celebrating the company's hundredth anniversary.

Then there was the late Stan Lee, former president and chairman of Marvel Comics and cocreator of Spider-Man, the Fantastic Four, and a host of other superheroes. Another lifelong White Castle fan from the Bronx, he was inducted into the White Castle Cravers Hall of Fame, along with Telfar, rocker Alice Cooper, and others.

Perhaps the most remarkable innovation came from a White Castle in Minneapolis. The manager there was familiar with all her regular customers, including a couple she knew would not be able to afford an expensive restaurant meal for the upcoming Valentine's Day. She offered to treat them to a meal at White Castle instead. When they came in, they found a table with a white cloth, flowers, and a reserved sign. The manager welcomed them, seated them at the table, and then waited on them while the other fast-food customers looked on in bewilderment and curiosity. The next Valentine's Day, she set up all her tables with white cloths and flowers and took reservations. It was an even bigger success. The following year, all the White Castles in Minneapolis did it. After that, all the restaurants did it, with reservations available on OpenTable. In 2020, White Castle had 36,000 reservations for February 14. If you wanted in, you'd need to make a reservation a year in advance.

Great Evergreens, as I was seeing repeatedly and especially at White Castle, sourced Pragmatic Innovation ideas from all levels of the organization. This Valentine's Day idea that has been so successful and positive for their brand arose from the creativity, kindness, and customer care of a store manager helping one customer. A manager who in turn must have felt deeply valued and supported by the company. Creativity doesn't happen in environments of fear or greed.

Tugboat Institute also welcomed the president and CEO of one of the largest private companies in America (sixteenth on the *Forbes* list): Rick Keyes of Meijer Inc., the family-owned chain of grocery stores and supercenters based in Grand Rapids, Michigan. Given its present size and influence, I was surprised to learn how the company had started. The founder was Hendrick Meijer, a Dutch immigrant in 1907, who spent years searching for a way to support himself and his future wife, eventually deciding to become a barber. He did reasonably well as a barber while continuing to try other ventures on the side.

One side hustle was real estate: he built two storefronts on property he owned next to his barbershop, figuring the units could provide him with steady rental income after he retired. It was 1934, however, the depths of the Great Depression, and he could find only one tenant. It occurred to him that the other unit was the right size for a corner grocery store, but none of the established grocers wanted it. For help in his search, he approached a grocery wholesaler, who suggested he open the store himself and offered to provide him, on credit, the inventory he would need to start. He accepted and opened North Side Grocery, ably assisted by his fourteen-year-old son Frederick, while continuing to pursue his career as a barber.

It happened to be an era of significant change in the grocery business. Corner grocery stores were giving way to supermarkets like A&P and Kroger, which offered lower prices and had an entirely different way of operating, including self-service, whereby customers, rather than a store clerk, chose the products they wanted and paid for them at checkout. The challenge led the Meijers to search for ways to compete against the chains by finding better products at lower prices, adopting self-service and other innovations, and opening additional stores. By the 1960s, they had fourteen stores in and around Grand Rapids.

Meanwhile, discount department stores such as Kmart and Dollar General were popping up. The Meijers thought that they could greatly enhance their grocery business by combining it with a discount store. A consultant suggested they set up their own discount outlet and lease out departments to specialized retailers in shoes, pharmacy, women's apparel, hardware, and other types of products. Such a project would obviously require more space, and so they decided to build a 100,000-square-foot building adjacent to one of their grocery stores.

It didn't take them long to discover that the nongrocery retailers didn't provide the same level of service, price, and quality that the Meijers insisted on. So they hired their own merchants to run the nongrocery businesses. The Meijers also realized that they needed only one checkout for the whole store, rather than a separate checkout for each department.

Thus, the supercenter was born. They called it Thrifty Acres.

The first one opened in 1962, and two more soon followed. One person who noticed was Sam Walton, who started Walmart that same year. Although not a direct competitor, Walton was well aware of the Meijers' business. In the late 1960s, Walton offered to buy Meijer, merge it with Walmart, and then go public. After Fred Meijer (now running it) declined, Walton went ahead and took Walmart public in 1970.

But he remembered Thrifty Acres and, in 1988, opened his version of such a store in Missouri—the first Walmart Supercenter of what would eventually become more than 3,500 nationwide. The

Meijer family also continued to open supercenters (now called simply "Meijer") in the six Midwestern states plus Kentucky where it competed. Interestingly, Walmart did not enter those markets until the last stages of its expansion—after it had opened supercenters everywhere else in the country. I don't know why Walmart delayed competing directly with Meijer, but it might have had something to do with the latter's strength in its markets. When Walmart finally did come in, they and Meijer were price competitive, but customers consistently ranked Meijer higher on quality and customer service.

In the beginning, of course, it wasn't clear that Meijer could survive the Walmart challenge. Indeed, throughout its history, the company has had to contend with one perilous situation after another. First, it was at risk of succumbing to A&P and Kroger, then later to Walmart, and then later still to Amazon. In every case, it managed not only to survive, but to emerge stronger than ever. The sturdiness and adaptivity that Evergreen companies create over decades serves them so well.

So, how *did* Meijer manage to thrive in the face of such competition?

The resourcefulness of the company's management surely played a role, but no factor was more important than the relationships Meijer had built over decades with customers, employees, and the wider community, backed up by the Meijer family, whose humility and generosity are legendary. The family gives more to philanthropy than it takes out for itself. That is, in fact, a rule for the business. In any year, more money must be given to philanthropy than the total distributed to owners.

I have never heard of *any* company that did that, let alone one that made it a rule. A public company wouldn't have the resources to do it, and if it did, it would kill the stock price. VC-backed ventures would have no patience for such a policy and private equity–backed firms zero out philanthropy, or keep just a modest level for PR value, essentially for virtue signaling.

Evergreens are just different. I was seeing it over and over again. It's telling that in 2024, thirty of Tugboat's member companies were at least a hundred years old. Their longevity was not merely incidental to their success. We ask all new members what they think was the most important source of competitive advantage for their Evergreen companies. People offer a variety of answers, but the most common one by far is the practice of taking the long view, a practice born out of the Evergreen 7Ps principles acting as a system.

I could readily appreciate how that perspective differentiated them from owners of other types of business. On average, the shareholders of public companies hold their stake for less than a year, and the companies are measured quarterly. Private equity investors want to be in and out in three years and monitor results monthly. So do venture capitalists, who plan to hold onto portfolio companies for five to seven years ideally before liquidating or distributing their shares. that is, the very longest view you get in the typical model is a decade, and a few more years in practice for the portfolio laggards. And here is O.C. Tanner, setting up one-hundred-year trusts.

There is no end date for owners of Evergreen companies. They never plan to exit, and so they are comfortable making decisions based on what they think is best for their companies in ten, twenty, or even a hundred years. In that sense, they are unique in the business world. Moreover, there are at least three other ways in which the long view gives them benefits.

Long view advantage 1: The compounding effect. I earlier noted how the compounding of revenue and profits over time leads to large and valuable companies. A company doing, say, $15 million in annual revenue that steadily grows an average of 15 percent per year, year after year, will be doing almost $1 billion annually in thirty years.

I had long understood financial compounding, but only later, and thanks to our members, did I come to appreciate how significantly time enables a similar compounding effect in *other* areas of the business besides revenue. As the decades pass, Evergreen companies experience dramatic strengthening and deepening of their cultures, teamwork, intellectual property, ability to innovate, operational efficiency, reputation and bonds with customers, and brands.

Long view advantage 2: Win-win partnerships. Evergreen companies do not play zero-sum games with other companies. Because they plan to be around forever, they strive for long-term win-win dynamics with their entire ecosystem. They expect, after all, to keep doing business with these other companies indefinitely, and so they want everyone to succeed.

The same can't be said of private equity, venture-backed, or public companies, all of which have owners that are not integral to the functioning of the underlying business and whose primary purpose is to maximize returns to themselves regardless whether that's in the best long-term interest of the company or its partners. A win for the owners may well lead to losses for someone else.

Public companies, for example, regularly give shareholders projections of future performance, but unforeseen conflicts may arise, threatening a company's ability to meet its goals. Its leaders are often so afraid of the market's reaction to missing the quarterly number that they'll lay off employees to achieve it. Private equity and venture capital firms, for their part, invariably prioritize what's ultimately going to lead to the highest-value exit in the shortest time frame possible. Those priorities often lead the firms they back to take dramatic actions even if they adversely affect employees, customers, and/or suppliers, and the long-term foundation of the business. I remember in my own experience at Good Technology scaling up the sales staff to hundreds of reps to meet aggressive growth goals. We had little data to suggest we could manage the sales process at such a scale, and inevitably we burned through tens of millions in cash and let nearly all those hires go.

Consider a typical venture-backed business. It is usually just one of fifty companies that have received capital from a given VC firm's fund, and it will often have capital from more than one venture firm. These firms all have different projected time frames and valuation expectations for the eventual exit, but things can take longer than expected, forcing them to extend their fund's time frame. As the VC firm is getting toward the tail end of its extension periods, its partners start looking for closure, especially if they have had big winners earlier in the fund. They reach a point at which they and their limited partners just want the fund to end. They say internally, "Let's find a reasonable exit and get on with it." At that point, the valuation doesn't matter so much. They just want to take that investment off the books. I remember several cases when VCs would say they didn't care if some company in their portfolio succeeded because they had some other big winner in their portfolio and no matter what happened with the firm in question, it wasn't going to move the needle on their fund. They'd almost brag that the company didn't matter to *their* success. They weren't thinking about the effect that their indifferent exit would have on the company they were leaving behind. However negative the consequences, the company's employees and customers would just have to cope. Once again, it's win-lose.

With private equity, the effect is even more pronounced because of the way PE deals are structured—typically with 2:1 debt to equity. Given all that leverage, the PE firm will push the company's management to do everything it can to enhance the short-term cash flow of the business whether by "reducing head count" (that is, layoffs), cutting high-paid positions, cutting back R&D investments, curtailing local philanthropy, reducing product quality and quantity, raising prices, or whatever. It's win-lose all the way.

In Evergreen companies, on the other hand, there are no exits or stock sales to external parties and thus no need to manipulate the financials for outsiders. During hard times, owners will tolerate lower distributions or even none at all. In the worst case, they will put money back into the company, as many did during the Covid crisis. The message is: we're in this together. We're building something that, over time, will have value to us all.

Paced Growth helps to make this possible. If your company is set up to grow 100 percent a year, a significant task of your job as CEO is to raise capital and add a lot of people. There's stress on the entire organization as half the team is new every year; the needs of current employees are ignored; and the culture suffers. But if the Paced Growth target is 10 percent to 20 percent a year, the company can absorb it in a way that reinforces the culture without exceeding its cash resources or management bandwidth. You have room to make sure that your customers are always getting the best product at a good price and your people are being well compensated, trained and developed, regularly recognized, and well led. I always go back to Wegmans, which could have easily added more stores a year, but chose to stick to only two. At the time, I saw this as leaving money on the table, as being too careful. I see now the discipline, the confidence of that decision. Sure, we could do that, but it adds risk, and we're going to be doing this for many decades to come. No need to chase every last dollar now.

Long view advantage 3: Fulfillment. This benefit was driven home to me by one of our members, Jim Milgard, the founder and CEO of Continental Floral Greens, the largest farm-to-market floral greens supplier in the United States. One night at dinner he said to me: "Dave, there's something about being a successful Evergreen CEO that other people will never understand," he said. "I'm talking about the way it feels. It's almost impossible to describe. The guys in venture-backed or private equity–owned companies have no idea what I'm talking about. They'll never experience it."

I had a sense of what he meant, but I wanted him to try to describe that feeling to me.

"It comes from getting to a point where you know your company is going to be around for the long haul. You have built a really stable base from your own profitability and growth," Milgard said. "It's knowing that your team is operating at a high level and working well together to the point where you can sit back and smile because of how well they are performing, coordinating, solving problems, supporting each other, and serving customers. It's about seeing your children care about the company's Purpose and team and having one of my daughters working in the business. It's just an incredible feeling of satisfaction and joy."

And that, I suppose, is the greatest reward of all.

The Evergreen 7Ps Principles

Seven Defining Characteristics of Evergreen Companies

1. Purpose: Having a compelling reason for existing—a North Star above all else.

2. Perseverance: Having the ambition and the resilience to overcome obstacles and keep pursuing the Purpose indefinitely into the future.

3. People First: Engaging a workforce of talented associates who excel as a team and are motivated by the Purpose and the culture, as well as by total compensation, in the belief that, by taking care of them, they will take care of the customers, suppliers, partners, communities, and their families.

4. Private: Taking advantage of the ability of closely held private companies to have a longer-term view, greater

confidentiality around strategies, and more operating flexibility than public or exit-oriented businesses.

5. Profit: Not mistaking profit as the purpose of the business, but recognizing it is essential to survival and independence, and the most accurate measure of customer value delivered.

6. Paced Growth: Having the discipline to focus on long-term strategy, balance short-term and long-term performance, and grow steadily and consistently from year to year.

7. Pragmatic Innovation: Embracing a continuous-improvement process built around taking calculated risks to innovate creatively within constraints.

An Evergreen Leader's Reading List

Here are thirty titles I recommend to all Tugboat Institute members, listed in alphabetical order by author. Each title includes inspiring ideas and lessons for Evergreen leaders and their companies.

It's Not about the Coffee: Lessons on Putting People First from a Life at Starbucks, Howard Behar with Janet Goldstein (New York: Portfolio, 2009)

Finish Big: How Great Entrepreneurs Exit Their Companies on Top, Bo Burlingham (New York: Portfolio, 2013)

The Power of Myth Interview Series, Joseph Campbell with Bill Moyers (PBS, 1988)

Creativity, Inc.: Overcoming the Unseen Forces That Stand in the Way of True Inspiration, Ed Catmull with Amy Wallace (New York: Random House, 2023)

Let My People Go Surfing: The Education of a Reluctant Businessman, Yvon Chouinard (New York: Penguin, 2016)

The Innovator's Dilemma: When New Technologies Cause Great Firms to Fail, Clayton M. Christensen (Boston: Harvard Business School Press, 1997)

Great by Choice: Uncertainty, Chaos, and Luck—Why Some Thrive Despite Them All, Jim Collins and Morten T. Hansen (New York: Harper Business, 2011)

Built to Last: Successful Habits of Visionary Companies, Jim Collins and Jerry I. Porras (New York: Harper Business, 1994)

Berkshire Beyond Buffett: The Enduring Value of Values, Lawrence A. Cunningham (New York: Columbia Business School Publishing, 2014)

The 15 Commitments of Conscious Leadership: A New Paradigm for Sustainable Success, Jim Dethmer, Diana Chapman, and Kaley Warner Klemp (published by the authors, 2015)

Measure What Matters: How Google, Bono, and the Gates Foundation Rock the World with OKRs, John Doerr (New York: Portfolio Penguin, 2018)

The Effective Executive: The Definitive Guide to Getting the Right Things Done, Peter Drucker (Hoboken, NJ: Harper Wiley, 2015)

Raised Healthy, Wealthy & Wise: Lessons from Successful and Grounded Inheritors on How They Got That Way, Coventry Edwards-Pitt (published by author, 2014)

Raising the Bar: Integrity and Passion in Life and Business: The Story of Clif Bar & Co.: A Journey Toward Sustaining Your

Business, Brand, People, Community, and the Planet, Gary Erickson with Lois Lorentzen (New York: Jossey-Bass, 2012)

The Heart of Business: Leadership Principles for the Next Era of Capitalism, Hubert Joly with Caroline Lambert (Boston: Harvard Business Review Press, 2021)

The Science of Success: How Market-Based Management Built the World's Largest Private Company, Charles G. Koch (Hoboken, NJ: Wiley, 2007)

The Advantage: Why Organizational Health Trumps Everything Else in Business, Patrick M. Lencioni (New York: Jossey-Bass, 2012)

Team of Teams: New Rules of Engagement for a Complex World, General Stanley McChrystal, Tantum Collins, David Silverman, and Chris Fussell (New York: Portfolio, 2015)

45 Effective Ways for Hiring Smart!: How to Predict Winners and Losers in the Incredibly Expensive People-Reading Game, Pierre Mornell and Regan Dunnick (Emeryville, CA: Ten Speed Press, 2011)

Poor Charlie's Almanack: The Essential Wit and Wisdom of Charles T. Munger, Charles T. Munger (San Francisco: Stripe Press, 2023)

Toyota Production System: Beyond Large-Scale Production, Taiichi Ohno (Boca Raton, FL: CRC Press, 1988)

The HP Way: How Bill Hewlett and I Built Our Company, David Packard (New York: Collins Business Essentials, 1995)

In Search of Excellence: Lessons from America's Best-Run Companies, Thomas J. Peters and Robert H. Waterman, Jr. (New York: Harper Business, 2006)

Only the Best Will Do: The Compelling Case for Investing in Quality Growth Businesses, Peter Seilern (Hampshire, UK: Harriman House, 2019)

Hidden Champions: Lessons from 500 of the World's Best Unknown Companies, Hermann Simon (Boston: Harvard Business School Press, 1996)

The Great Game of Business: The Only Sensible Way to Run a Company, Jack Stack with Bo Burlingham (New York: Doubleday/Currency, 1992)

No Man's Land: Where Growing Companies Fail, Doug Tatum (New York: Portfolio, 2008)

The Outsiders: Eight Unconventional CEOs and Their Radically Rational Blueprint for Success, William H. Thorndike (Boston: Harvard Business Review Press, 2012)

Rocket Fuel: The One Essential Combination That Will Get You More of What You Want from Your Business, Gino Wickman and Mark C. Winters (Dallas: BenBella Books, 2015)

The End of the World Is Just the Beginning: Mapping the Collapse of Globalization, Peter Zeihan (New York: Harper Business, 2022)

Continue Your Evergreen Journey

Information and Resources for Readers to Continue Their Learning Journey

We hope this book has offered a meaningful perspective into the journey that led me to discover and celebrate these extraordinary Evergreen leaders and companies. My genuine intention in sharing this story is to elevate awareness and appreciation of the Evergreen companies making a difference in every community and across the globe. I hope it inspires the best in all of us.

We'd love to hear from you—whether you have a success story or a fresh idea, are interested in membership, or simply have some feedback to share. Please feel free to reach out to us at share@tugboatinstitute.com. We read every email and respond to most. This is not a gimmick either, we promise.

We hope your Evergreen journey doesn't end here. We invite you to explore further and continue your path of growth and learning.

Resources from Tugboat Institute

Visit our Tugboat Institute website for more information: www .tugboatinstitute.com.

Sign up for our free weekly Evergreen Journal newsletter spotlighting wisdom and insights from our Evergreen Community: https://evergreenjournal.com.

Follow us to get more ideas, best practices, inspiration, and thought leadership: Tugboat Institute's LinkedIn page (https://www .linkedin.com/company/tugboat-institute/) and Dave Whorton's LinkedIn profile (https://www.linkedin.com/in/davewhorton/).

INDEX

ACKNOWLEDGMENTS

This book would not exist without Bo Burlingham. His October 2015 *Inc.* magazine article, "How to Build a Company That Will Be Around in 2115," provided important validation and has been a cornerstone reference for Tugboat Institute and Evergreen leaders. Bo also introduced me to Jack Stack, founder and CEO of SRC Holdings, whose friendship and guidance has had an immense positive impact on me, often at key junctures. Finally, Bo's offer to coauthor this book, despite the fact that I'm an engineer by training and an inexperienced writer, made this entire process a joy. His approach—conducting interviews at Sun Valley Inn for long hours over several days and turning select stories into beautiful prose—made this book what it is.

Many thanks to Spencer Burke, Scott Carlin, Mel Gravely, Tina Hrevus, John Jennings, Rick Keyes, Roberta Katz, Penny Pennington, Dave Petersen, Jeff Snipes, Lisa Whorton, and Rylee Whorton for reading early drafts of the manuscript and offering detailed, valuable feedback.

Daniel Greenberg embraced our unconventional approach of finishing the first draft before seeking publishers, ultimately bringing us together with Harvard Business Review Press.

A special, heartfelt thanks to Scott Berinato, our exceptional editor at the Press. From our first meeting, where Scott shared his love and passion for narrative stories, I knew he was the one and that we would be in good hands. His masterful editing made the book even better, and his warmth and quick wit made every meeting a pleasure. Thanks too to the entire HBR Press team for producing this book, bringing it to bookshelves, and promoting it wisely.

Finally, I am grateful to my team at Tugboat Institute for their patience and support throughout this five-year book journey.

—Dave Whorton

ABOUT THE AUTHORS

DAVE WHORTON is the founder of Tugboat Institute, where his and the firm's Purpose is to help entrepreneurs and leaders build enduring, purpose-driven, people-first, profitable, growth companies and to have Tugboat Institute itself be an Evergreen exemplar. When he's not championing the cause of Evergreen companies, you might find him chasing his next big idea for them, debating whether his third or fourth coffee should be regular or decaf, or enjoying a hike in Idaho's Sawtooth Mountains. Dave brings a blend of wisdom, wit, perseverance, and a whole lot of heart to everything he does. His journey from Silicon Valley entrepreneur and venture capitalist to Evergreen company visionary has made him a trusted friend and valuable resource to leaders of Evergreen businesses that last and last and last.

BO BURLINGHAM has been writing about entrepreneurs and entrepreneurship for the past forty-five years, mostly for *Inc.* magazine, where he served as executive editor and then editor-at-large. He has also written for *Forbes*, *Esquire*, and *Harper's*, among other publications. Along the way, he has authored five books, including *Small Giants: Companies That Choose to Be Great Instead of Big*, which was a finalist for the Financial Times and Goldman Sachs Business Book of the Year award. He has written three other books with coauthors, including two with Jack Stack, CEO of SRC Holdings Corporation. The first of these, *The Great Game of*

Business, is widely considered to be one of 100 best business books of all time. He also wrote *Street Smarts: An All-Purpose Tool Kit for Entrepreneurs* with Norm Brodsky, founder of CitiStorage and many other companies.